Language Arts Thinking Motivators

by
Thomas J. Palumbo

illustrated by Bron Smith

Cover by Vanessa Filkins

Copyright © Good Apple, Inc., 1988

Good Apple, Inc.
Box 299
Carthage, IL 62321-0299

TH from Beginning to End
Blank Master

The first clue will form a word with _____ (your selected letters) in a variety of different positions. The second clue will give you the word that remains after _____ is removed.

Clues	Answers
1.	
2.	
3.	
4.	
5.	
6.	
7.	
8.	
9.	
10.	
11.	
12.	
13.	
14.	
15.	

A. How many words did you find on your own?_____

B. How many did friends help you with? _____ Parents? _____

C. In what sources did you find your words?_____

_____ _____

Consecutive Letters Cross Out

If you correctly cross out two letters that are consecutive in each word below, you will leave an easy-to-recognize new word. Some words will have mulitple answers.

Multiple Word	Letter Pairs Out	Word(s)
Example: Stripe	st	ripe
1. Today		
2. Pelican		
3. Steamer		
4. Attract		
5. Students		
6. Muscle		
7. Balance		
*8. Weapon		
9. Grenade		
10. Scared		
11. Discord		
12. Battle		
13. Monarch		
14. Mellow		
15. Justice		
16. Chariot		

Can you find five words that have the same characteristic?

1. _____ _____ _____

2. _____ _____ _____

3. _____ _____ _____

4. _____ _____ _____

5. _____ _____ _____

Measure a Word
Vocabulary and Spelling Drill
Student Page

The following clues are given for words that rhyme with measurement words. Find the clue words and the measurement words; then write and complete the appropriate problems.

Clue	Word	Measurement	Problem
1. I'm the opposite of sweet.	Sour	Hour	4 x 4 = 16
2. The recipe calls for this much salt.			
3. I sell rings and watches.			
4. I'm a green fruit like a lemon.			
5. I'm a Peter Paul candy bar.			
6. I'm a relative of yours.			
7. I'm what you play poker with.			
8. I'm a person who copies a test.			
9. I'm what a ball does.			
10. I'm where soldiers fight Indians.			
11. I'm a shout of joy.			
12. I shine at night.			
13. I'm a young dog.			
14. I bake cakes.			
15. I'm the word that tells you to get lost.			
16. I'm the black stuff in a chimney.			
17. I'm something children like to do.			
18. I'm a stack of things.			

Measure a Word
Vocabulary and Spelling Drill
Teacher Directions

Purpose: To give rhyming word practice.
           To review measurement vocabulary.

Place this clue on the chalkboard: I'm the opposite of sweet. | sour hour |

    Ask if anyone knows the answer. Place the answer **sour** next to the clue. Then inform the class that the answer to the clue will help you to find a measurement word that rhymes with **sour**. Place the class answer **hour** next to **sour**. Write their answer under each word with a times sign in between. Ask the class for the answer.

              sour   hour
           4 x 4 = 16

    The following clues are given for words that rhyme with measurement words. Challenge the class to find the clue words and the measurement words that would go next to them. Then write and complete the appropriate problem. The clues can be given orally or on the work sheet.

Clue	Word	Measurement	Problem
1. I'm the opposite of sweet.	Sour	Hour	4 x 4 = 16
2. The recipe calls for this much salt.	Pinch	Inch	5 x 4 = 20
3. I sell rings and watches.	Jeweler	Ruler	7 x 5 = 35
4. I'm a green fruit like a lemon.	Lime	Time	4 x 4 = 16
5. I'm a Peter Paul candy bar.	Mounds	Pounds	6 x 6 = 36
6. I'm a relative of yours.	Cousin	Dozen	6 x 5 = 30
7. I'm what you play poker with.	Cards	Yards	5 x 5 = 25
8. I'm a person who copies a test.	Cheater	Meter	7 x 5 = 35
9. I'm what a ball does.	Bounce	Ounce	6 x 5 = 30
10. I'm where soldiers fight Indians.	Fort	Quart	4 x 5 = 20
11. I'm a shout of joy.	Cheer	Year	5 x 4 = 20
12. I shine at night.	Moon	Spoon	4 x 5 = 20
13. I'm a young dog.	Pup	Cup	3 x 3 = 9
14. I bake cakes.	Baker	Acre	5 x 4 = 20
15. I'm the word that tells you to get lost.	Scram	Gram	5 x 4 = 20
16. I'm the black stuff in a chimney.	Soot	Foot	4 x 4 = 16
17. I'm something children like to do.	Play	Day	4 x 3 = 12
18. I'm a stack of things.	Pile	Mile	4 x 4 = 16

Have the class pick some themes of their own. Remind them to record the problems.

Examples:

Food	Ice Cream	3 x 5 = 15
Cars	Ford Mustang	4 x 7 = 28
Rhymers	Fat Cat	3 x 3 = 9
Sports	Philadelphia Phillies	12 x 8 = 96
TV Programs	*Charlie's Angels*	8 x 6 = 48

Metric Words

This is a nice follow-up to "Measure a Word." All words that have exactly ten letters are called "metric words."

The clues given below will help you find "metric words." After you find an answer, record a classmate's answer that you didn't discover in the second column.

Clue	Your Answer	A Classmate's Answer
Example: A bird	Woodpecker	_____
1. A U.S. state	_____	_____
2. A country	_____	_____
3. A boy's name	_____	_____
*4. A girl's name	_____	_____
5. A U.S. city	_____	_____
6. A travel vehicle	_____	_____
*7. A character from history	_____	_____
8. Lincoln and Washington	_____	_____
9. Daily news and inquirer	_____	_____
*10. The earth's spin around sun	_____	_____
*11. A sport	_____	_____
*12. Room temperature regulator	_____	_____

Can you find five additional "metric words"?

1._____

2._____

3._____

4._____

5._____

Give Me Three, Four, Five or Six
Student Page

Examine the category on the left. Try to find a three, four, five and six-letter word for each category. Circle each answer that has a long vowel sound in it as you complete the chart below.

Category	Three-Letter	Four-Letter	Five-Letter	Six-Letter
Farm Animal	(Ewe) Pig	(Goat)	Horse	(Donkey)
Vegetable				
Fish				
Boy				
Girl				
Body of Water				
Fruit				
Tree				
Plant/Flower				
Metals				
Beverages				
Desserts				
Bird				
Clothing	(Tie)	Sock	Shirt	Shorts
*				
*				

*Pick two categories of your own and complete the chart.

Give Me Three, Four, Five, or Six
Teacher Directions

This activity will develop classification, research, long vowel and spelling skills. Tell your pupils that they are going on a word hunt. The words they will be looking for will have only three letters. Ask them to look at themselves and around the room to see if they can find things with three letters (pen, arm, leg, eye). Place the chart below on the chalkboard and tell the class you will continue the hunt for three-letter words.

	Short Vowel	Long Vowel
Boy's Name		
Girl's Name		
Body Part		
Mineral		
Game		
Color		

Let's see if we as a class can find a long and short vowel word for each category above. Start with three-letter words and then move to the pupil page. The ability of your class will determine which columns they would complete on the student page.

Possible Answers

Category	Three-Letter	Four-Letter	Five-Letter	Six-Letter
Farm Animal	Ewe, Pig	Goat	Horse	Donkey
Vegetable	Pea	Bean	Onion	Carrot
Fish	Eel	Carp	Trout	Minnow
Boy	Ben	Mike	Peter	Sydney
Girl	Amy	Jean	Monet	Joanie
Body of Water	Sea	Lake	Ocean	Stream
Fruit	Fig	Lime	Grape	Tomato
Tree	Oak	Pine	Maple	Walnut
Plant/Flower	Ivy	Rose	Tulip	Violet
Metals	Tin	Iron	Steel	Cobalt
Beverages	Tea	Coke	Juice	Coffee
Desserts	Pie	Cake	Jell-O	Cookie
Bird	Owl	Crow	Robin	Turkey
Clothing	Tie	Sock	Shirt	Shorts

21

Checkerboard Challenge
Long Vowels
Student Page

The checkerboard is a natural teaching device. Most children are familiar with the board and the moves necessary to play. Give every two players a cube with the vowels (A E I O U A) on it. Pieces of paper with vowels written on them will also work. Clear Bingo chips make good movers.

	Repay		Ride		Potato		Mile
Please		Rain		Snow		Silo	
	Polite		Amy		Usual		Huge
Bicycle		Human		Pony		Jeans	
	Giant		Ice		Ace		Go
Irene		Ohio		Stain		Treat	
	Like		Unite		See		Idaho
Steam		Oleo		Halo		Tomato	

A   **B**   **C**   **D**

Place your team's marker on a letter above. Throw your vowel cube and move to the word that has the long vowel sound. Your next throw must decode into one of the two choices directly above your marker or you can't move. The first one that reaches the top line wins. Alternate throws. Can you design a checkerboard game using the blank master?

Checkerboard Challenge
Blank Master

Use this checkerboard to design an activity of your own. Any skill can be reinforced in a similar fashion to the one you've practiced (vowel sounds).

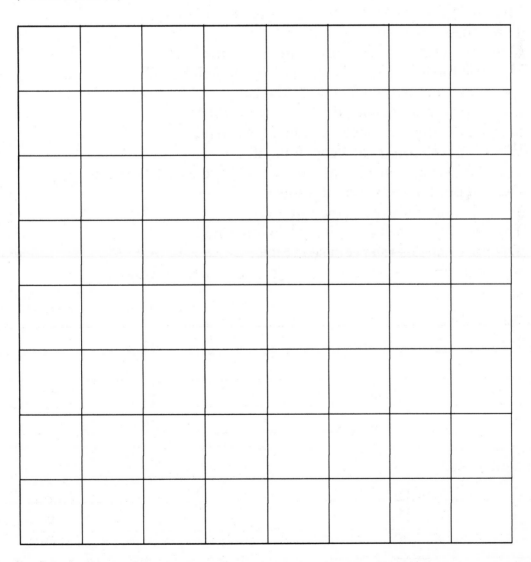

Carol Stemrich's Compounds

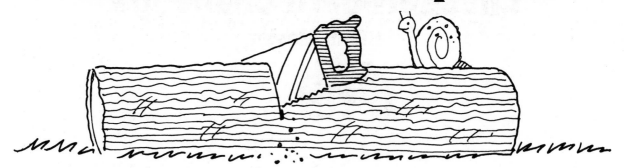

Each sentence contains at least two words that can be put together to form a compound word. Underline these words and record them below. Multiply the number of letters in each word to find your score. Write three sentences which will allow us to search for your answers.

1. Did you **see** him **saw** that log?
2. She could not find her coat anywhere in the house.
3. The house has a pine tree in front of it.
4. One day I want to visit every store in the mall.
5. How will the light show off that painted Indian head?
6. He wanted to hold the film up to the light.
7. It is your turn to go over the homework tonight.
8. Please put some of those peanuts in my hand.
9. What time do you go to sleep at night?
10. Try *The Yearling*, just in case you don't have a book to read.
11. Did she put the toy set on the shelf?
12. We will go to the store some other day.
13. The doctor is a master at fixing broken arms.
14. The port handles river and sea traffic.
15. My mother always finds a way to get me to walk to school.

1. <u>seesaw   3 x 3 = 9</u>
2. _____
3. _____
4. _____
5. _____

6. _____
7. _____
8. _____
9. _____
10. _____

11. _____
12. _____
13. _____
14. _____
15. _____

Your sentences:

1. _____
2. _____
3. _____

The Union and Intersection of Compound Words

The intersection of a compound word is where the two words meet (last letter, first word; first letter, second word). Each group of letters below is missing the intersection (two letters) that would make it a compound word. How many can you solve?

Word Fragment	Intersection	Union
Example: Housife	ew	Housewife
1. Basall		
2. Scarrow		
3. Beoom		
4. Everody		
*5. Iide		
*6. Altar		
7. Teeger		
8. Holp		
9. Sehore		
10. Sidalk		
11. Trut		
12. Uet		
13. Tablloth		
14. Turver		
15. Firan		

Can you write three problems of your own?

1. _____   _____   _____

2. _____   _____   _____

3. _____   _____   _____

Letter Loader

The Letter Loader Company lends out its trucks to people that are interested in improving their spelling. Cut out the boxes below and load them on the truck in correct order as your teacher calls out spelling words. Can you find ten, four-letter words using the boxes below? This can also be used for initial or final consonant drills. If you also teach math, white out the letters and replace them with numbers before giving this sheet to your students. You can then practice place value or the answers to addition, subtraction, multiplication and division problems.

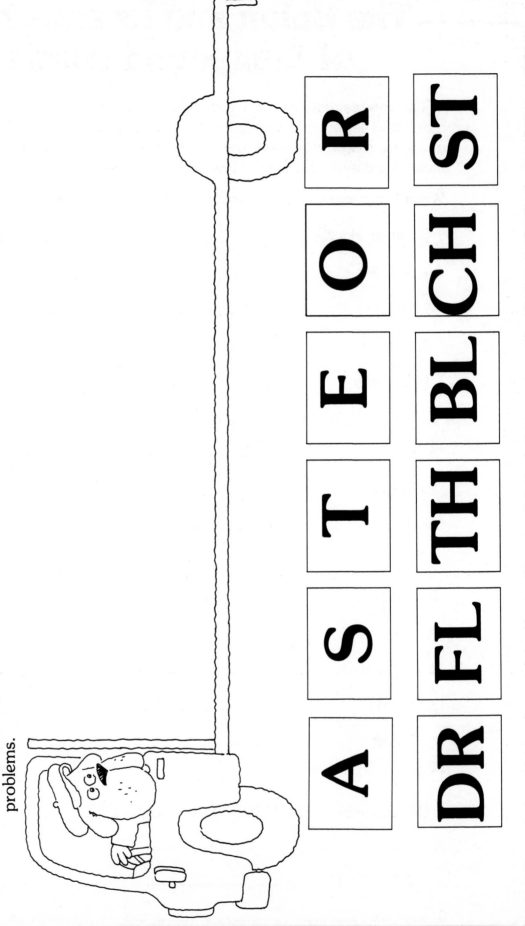

| A | S | T | E | O | R |
| DR | FL | TH | BL | CH | ST |

Across Words Puzzle I

This is a new type of seek-and-find. Each line across the chart below contains a number of words. Two of the words are opposite in meaning. Find the words and record them below. Color in the first letter of each word. The number above each first letter is your word's value. Add and record the values of the antonyms you find.

	1	2	3	4	5	6	7	8	9	10	11	12	13
Example:	N	A	G	L	A	D	O	T	S	A	D	Y	E
1.	S	O	N	G	O	T	O	F	F	E	E	V	E
2.	A	T	H	E	A	D	E	A	F	O	O	T	O
3.	B	A	T	W	I	N	C	L	O	S	E	A	M
4.	O	N	E	I	F	A	T	A	L	L	E	A	N
5.	H	A	S	I	P	E	G	U	L	P	O	R	E
6.	C	U	P	O	N	D	O	W	N	E	R	E	D
7.	B	R	A	G	L	O	V	E	H	A	T	E	R
8.	F	A	D	A	D	A	M	A	S	T	E	V	E
9.	P	A	I	D	A	S	H	U	R	T	A	R	P
10.	L	E	N	D	O	R	O	B	E	G	I	N	K
11.	S	P	I	N	T	S	T	O	U	T	A	G	O
12.	C	A	P	R	I	D	E	W	A	L	K	E	G

Example: <u>Glad</u> <u>Sad</u> <u>3 + 9 = 12</u>

1. ___ ___ ___   7. ___ ___ ___
2. ___ ___ ___   8. ___ ___ ___
3. ___ ___ ___   9. ___ ___ ___
4. ___ ___ ___   10. ___ ___ ___
5. ___ ___ ___   11. ___ ___ ___
6. ___ ___ ___   12. ___ ___ ___

Across Words Puzzle II

Each line across the chart below contains a number of words. Two of the words are synonyms. Find and record them below. Color in the first letter of each word. The values above these letters should then be multiplied and recorded. The words are written left to right or right to left.

	1	2	3	4	5	6	7	8	9	10	11	12	13
Example:	H	A	M	A	N	E	L	A	M	A	R	T	S
1.	P	E	E	L	T	T	I	L	L	A	M	S	T
2.	A	S	P	R	E	S	E	N	T	S	N	O	W
3.	I	T	S	A	O	B	R	A	G	O	L	D	O
4.	H	O	T	L	E	B	O	R	P	A	R	T	S
5.	S	L	O	O	P	A	L	O	N	E	V	E	R
6.	P	L	E	A	D	E	T	C	E	R	I	D	E
7.	O	F	F	A	T	E	S	E	B	O	R	N	O
8.	E	L	A	E	S	H	U	T	T	E	R	M	S
9.	I	T	E	S	Y	D	A	E	R	I	C	O	B
10.	B	A	N	U	F	L	I	P	A	S	S	O	T
11.	A	M	I	L	S	O	N	I	H	T	R	A	P
12.	M	E	S	A	E	L	O	R	E	N	T	O	N

Example: __Man__ __Male__ 3 x 9 = 27

1. _____ _____ _____

2. _____ _____ _____

3. _____ _____ _____

4. _____ _____ _____

5. _____ _____ _____

6. _____ _____ _____

7. _____ _____ _____

8. _____ _____ _____

9. _____ _____ _____

10. _____ _____ _____

11. _____ _____ _____

12. _____ _____ _____

Across Words Puzzle
Blank Master

Hide your own synonyms among other letters in the boxes below. The words should be written left to right or right to left. Exchange your sheet with a classmate. Color in the first letter of each word. Figure your own score.

	1	2	3	4	5	6	7	8	9	10	11	12	13
1.													
2.													
3.													
4.													
5.													
6.													
7.													
8.													
9.													
10.													
11.													
12.													

1. _____ _____ _____
2. _____ _____ _____
3. _____ _____ _____
4. _____ _____ _____
5. _____ _____ _____
6. _____ _____ _____

7. _____ _____ _____
8. _____ _____ _____
9. _____ _____ _____
10. _____ _____ _____
11. _____ _____ _____
12. _____ _____ _____

Said and Donne

John Donne used the word **yesternight** in his poem "Song." It is a pretty but archaic word that Samuel Johnson defines as "on the night of yesterday, last night." See if you can research a source for archaic words and record ten of the best (word and definition) on the chart below.

Example: a. Twain-two _____   n. _____

b. _____   o. _____

c. _____   p. _____

d. _____   q. _____

e. _____   r. _____

f. _____   s. _____

g. _____   t. _____

h. _____   u. _____

i. _____   v. _____

j. _____   w. _____

k. _____   x. _____

l. _____   y. _____

m. _____   z. _____

Which word above is your favorite? _____

Did any of your words appear on another person's list?

_____ _____ _____ _____

Lear Limerick Lore I

Edwin Lear (1812-1888) is known as the Father of the Modern Limerick because of the way he popularized its use and form.

> There once was an artist named Lear
> Who wrote verses to make children cheer.
> Though they never made sense,
> Their success was immense,
> And the Queen thought Lear was a dear.
> H. I. Brock.

A. What would a description of yourself look like in limerick form? Record it below.

_____

_____

_____

_____

_____

B. Pick a political, sport, entertainment or family figure and describe him/her in a limerick.

_____

_____

_____

_____

_____

C. Can you find an example of a humorous limerick and record it here?

_____

_____

_____

_____

_____

Teacher Note: Before this mini unit, discuss the limerick's rhyme scheme (A, A, B, B, A) with your class. Check your library for other limerick examples your class might enjoy before beginning these activities.

Lear Limerick Lore II

The "Learic" (Edwin Lear never used the word **limerick**) had endless possibilities for surprise, humor and wit. After reading many of the famous writers of limericks, you may agree that it is a shame that most people associate bawdiness with limericks. They were, indeed, a fascinating literary form. It is rewarding to see that many limerick writers also focused on the teaching aspect of their art form.

A goddess capricious is Fame.
You may strive to make noted your name.
But she either neglects you
Or coolly selects you
For laurels distinct from your aim.
                                        Langford Reed

There was a young student from Grime
Who thought that **one** was a prime.
It took a good teacher
To finally reach her
And now one's **unique** all the time.
                                        Thomas J. Palumbo

Compose two teaching limericks in the spaces below. Try to vary the subjects you select.

A. _____

_____

_____

_____

_____

B. _____

_____

_____

_____

_____

GRIME
SCHOOL

Lear Limerick Lore III

Queen Victoria selected Edward Lear as her drawing master because of his success as a commercial artist. His *Book of Nonsense* (1846) highlighted his original illustrations and verses. Illustrate the two limericks below; then compose and illustrate one of your own. *Please use the other side of this page to center your limerick and illustrations.

A. A scientist living at Staines
    In searching with infinite pains
    For a new type of sound
    Which he hopes, when it's found,
    Will travel much faster than planes.

B. I wish that my room had a floor;
    I don't care so much for a door;
    But this walking around
    Without touching the ground
    Is getting to be quite a bore.

                                    Gelett Burgess

Lear Limerick Lore IV

An early 1500's *Irish bartender used the limerick to advertise his trade. Perhaps we can start a limerick revival by showing various advertisers that a limerick campaign would benefit their products.

> * I sell the best brandy and sherry
> To make good customers merry;
> But at times their finances
> Run short, as it chances,
> And then I feel very sad, very.
>
> John O'Tuomy

A. Wendys' "Where's the beef?" campaign was a huge success. Can you create a limerick that would advertise their hamburger (food) business?

_____

_____

_____

_____

_____

B. Select a product of your own and team it with an original limerick.

_____

_____

_____

_____

_____

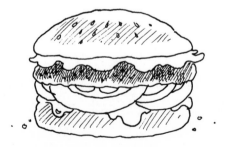

Just Desserts

Each character below has a favorite dessert. Some characteristic of his/her life will give you a clue to that person's favorite cake, pie or pudding.

Clue	**Dessert**
Example: A teacher uses on the blackboard	Chocolate Pudding

1. George Washington _____

2. Satan _____

3. A boat rower _____

4. A star gazer _____

5. Ghengis Khan _____

6. Truck driver/Furniture mover _____

7. Little Jack Horner _____

8. William Tell _____

9. Queen of Hearts _____

10. Heavenly people _____

11. Weight lifter _____

12. Neil Armstrong, moon walker _____

13. Bugs Bunny _____

14. Mr. Scrooge, sourpuss _____

15. Shoemaker _____

Can you design three clues of your own?

1. _____

2. _____

3. _____

Win or Lose

Each clue will give you a word that has **win** or **lose** in it. The letters in **win** and **lose** appear in exact order in the answers you discover.

Clue	Word
Example: A season	<u>Winter</u>

1. Opposite of far   _____

2. Eye movement   _____

3. A drink   _____

4. Look-alikes   _____

5. Place for hanging clothes   _____

6. Vital airplane part   _____

7. Opposite of open   _____

8. Picture taken near you   _____

9. A backyard ride   _____

10. Panes are found there   _____

11. To cheat   _____

12. _____ *in the Willows* (Book)   _____

13. Farmer's water pump   _____

14. Castle of Royal Family   _____

15. Capital of Manitoba, Canada   _____

Use the back of this page for three "win or lose" word clues? Challenge us.

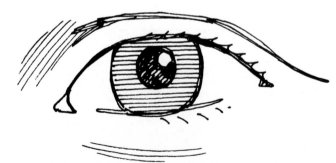

Picture Poetry

Student Page

Select a poem and copy it on this page.

Title of Poem _____ Author _____

Find a picture that represents the poem. Cut the picture in half and place it on the left-hand side of this page. You may use a larger sheet of paper if you need it. Draw the right-hand side of the picture with colored pencils. Record the relationship of your picture to the poem.

Picture	Drawn Half

Relationship . . . _____

_____

_____

Picture Poetry
Teacher Directions

Discuss the phrase "a picture paints a thousand words" with your class. If this is true, what about a poet's words . . . shouldn't the words paint a picture?

Explain to the class that they will select a poem and then find a picture that is representative of the poem. They will mount one half of the picture on the student page. The second half of the picture will be drawn. It can be a copy of the real second half or an addition to it by the student. After the picture is completed, the relationship between the picture and the poem should be detailed on the student page. You may want to have each student make a three-part mural with poem, picture and relationship side by side.

Square Abouts
Student Page

Below you will find hidden words in each square. Each word contains nine letters, the last of which appears in the middle of each square. The beginning of each word should be found. Then decide whether to walk clockwise or counterclockwise around the square ending with the middle square's letter. Record your answers below.

Example:

P	O	C
T	E	S
E	L	E

1.
E	S	R
C	Y	A
R	E	T

2.
O	T	A
E	R	L
S	C	A

3.
E	R	R
G	R	I
U	L	A

4.
E	S	A
P	D	H
U	R	C

5.
P	E	R
O	N	A
O	I	T

6.
O	R	A
O	F	I
R	P	N

7.
N	I	M
A	E	I
T	E	L

8.
R	E	S
D	S	H
D	A	E

9.
T	H	W
R	D	A
A	E	R

10.
I	R	O
T	E	E
M	E	T

Example: _Telescope_

1. _____
2. _____
3. _____
4. _____
5. _____

6. _____
7. _____
8. _____
9. _____
10. _____

Square Abouts
Blank Master

Fill in your own words and exchange this sheet with your classmates.

1.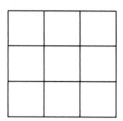

2.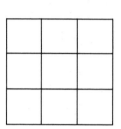

3.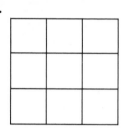

4.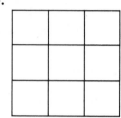

5.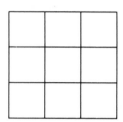

6.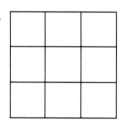

7.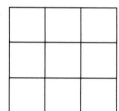

8.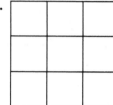

9.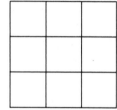

10.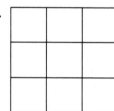

11.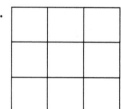

1. _____

2. _____

3. _____

4. _____

5. _____

6. _____

7. _____

8. _____

9. _____

10. _____

11. _____

40

Video Review Card Catalogue

Some people think that videos will be the literature of the future. Your library card catalog will be a video file instead of a book index. After watching a video (VCR tape), fill out the form below which will be incorporated with your classmates' selections into a viewing recommendation index.

Name of Video _____ Rating (if movie)_____

Type of Video (circle) Movie   Documentary   Instructional   Cartoon

Music   Comedy   Other _____

Director _____

Principal Characters_____

Description of Video for Future Viewers

_____

_____

Creative Aspects of the Video

_____

_____

What you would change to make it more creative?

_____

_____

Overall Recommendation

_____

_____

Long Vowel Contact
Gameboard

Materials: Two cubes lettered with A, E, I, O, U, ✱ (meaning free vowel)

Object: Throw the two cubes; select one or both of the outcomes and color the appropriate matching long vowel word on the activity board below.

Scoring: Score one point for each marker you touch that has been previously played; if both letters thrown are long sounds in your word, the score is doubled; teams alternate throwing cubes over nine innings.

OBOE	EVIL	LEVI	PANE	OKAY
MULE	UNITE	TINY	LEEWAY	TEPEE
OREO	GROWN	GO	BUTTE	FUEL
FATE	SERENE	MEAN	OHIO	COAT
JOKER	UTE	TRAINEE	LOGO	REUSE
REPAY	TRIO	LOCATE	KITE	GRAY
BABY	BONUS	YEAST	SCENIC	PROFANE
DETAIN	HUGE	OLEO	LEAF	BEET
LEAN	SEASIDE	YOUTH	HUMANE	TREATY
BOWLING	UNIQUE	BOLD	FINE	SAVE

Team 1

Team 2

Memory Writing

Alfred Lord Tennyson in his poem *In Memoriam* states in one stanza:

> Ring out, wild bells, to the wild sky
> The flying cloud, the frosty light:
> This year is dying in the night,
> Ring out, wild bells, and let him die.

1. Can you compose an "In Memoriam" which will highlight some of your personal memories from last year?

2. Can you write the pro and con arguments for the statement made in the poem that **we should let memories die?**

Why We Should Let Memories Die	Why We Should Not Let Memories Die

It Is a Bull Market

Your stock will increase $9 for each answer that you get correct. You're to find answers that have **bull** in them. The hints will help you. The starting price for your stock is $23.

Hint	Answer	Increase	Stock's Value
Example: A Civil War Battle	Bull Run	_____	_____
1. Found in a gun	_____	_____	_____
2. Spanish sport	_____	_____	_____
3. Gold or silver bar	_____	_____	_____
4. European bird	_____	_____	_____
5. A stubborn person	_____	_____	_____
6. A croaker	_____	_____	_____
7. A type of vest	_____	_____	_____
8. A place for office notices	_____	_____	_____
9. Construction equipment	_____	_____	_____
10. A baseball term	_____	_____	_____
11. A type of dog	_____	_____	_____
12. Teddy Roosevelt's party	_____	_____	_____
13. A target	_____	_____	_____
14. Type of fish	_____	_____	_____

How many problems did you get correct? _____

What was the final price of your stock? _____

What percent did your stock increase by? _____

How did you determine this? _____

_____

_____

44

Building a Better House

Each clue below will help you to find a word (or words) that begins or ends with **house**. Your score is determined by squaring the letters to the left or right of **house**.

Hint	Answer	Score
Example: A woman servant	House**maid**	4 x 4 = 16
1. A house insect	_____	_____
2. A farm bathroom	_____	_____
3. A bathroom-trained pet	_____	_____
4. A type of kitchen robe	_____	_____
5. Storage place for oars, etc.	_____	_____
6. A government body (U.S.A.)	_____	_____
7. Kitchen supplies	_____	_____
8. Large storage building	_____	_____
9. Good for river travel and sleeping	_____	_____
10. A Roman washing place	_____	_____
11. A backyard place for children	_____	_____
12. All the people living in a home	_____	_____
13. A person hired to do housework	_____	_____
14. Another name for a fire station	_____	_____
15. Bartender's words for free	_____	_____
16. A ship's near-danger helper	_____	_____
17. A government body (England)	_____	_____
18. An outdoor brightener for the home	_____	_____

Facial Analysis
Student Page

Cut out the frontal view of a person's face. Cut the face in half. Place the left part of the face in Figure 1 below and draw the right-hand side with colored pencils. Place the right-hand side of the face in the right side of Figure 2. On the left side of Figure 2 put your description or analysis of that person. You may want to use a large piece of paper or two sheets, if necessary.

First Half of Face   **Drawn Second Half of Face**

Figure 1

Facial Analysis   **Second Half of Face**

Figure 2

Facial Analysis
Teacher Directions

You may want to discuss the phrases

"the face that launched a thousand ships"
"love at first sight"
"I knew you as soon as I saw you"

with the class before starting this activity. A trip to a portrait section of a local museum or looking at portraits in an art book are good prerequisites to this activity. Tell the class to cut out two frontal views of people (one of someone they know and one of an unknown person). After they cut the face in half and paste it on the student page, have them draw the second half as close as possible to the original. You may change this to drawing the second half completely different from the first half. The second half of the activity will test your ability to figure people out from their pictures. When you analyze the person you know, don't put down things everyone knows but put your original analysis of that person. This activity is a real attention getter when put on large paper on a bulletin board display.

47

Facial Analysis

Blank Master

Place half of a cutout face on the left side of this page. Draw the right side completely different.

Face	Drawn Side

Circle World
Student Page

Listen to your teacher's directions for the secret that should be placed in circles 1, 2, 3, 4, and 5. Complete each circle with answers for each category.

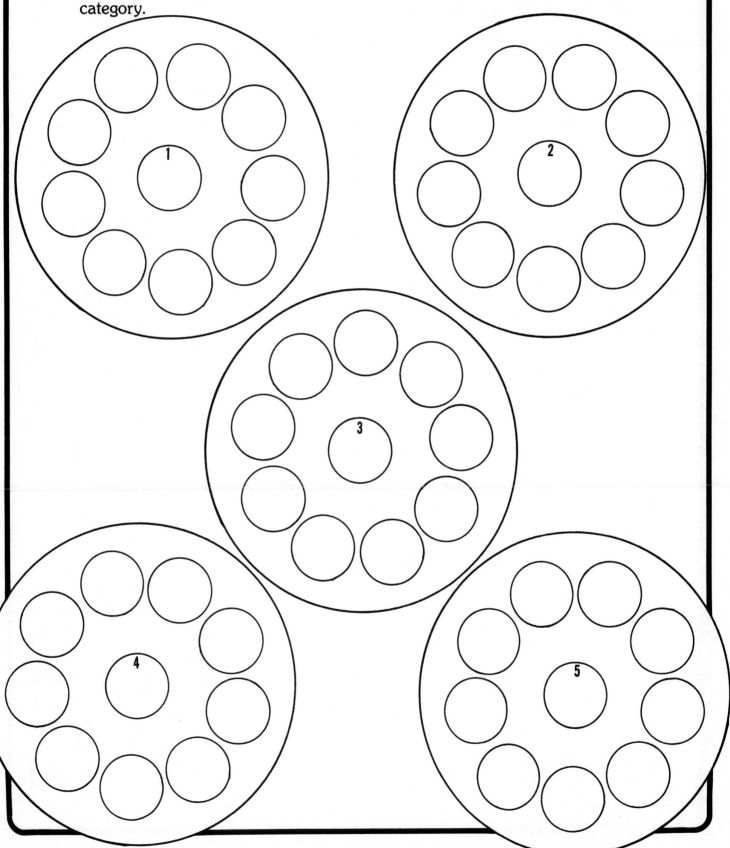

Circle World
Teacher Page

There are very few concepts in language arts that cannot be reinforced by using "Circle World." The student page is blank so you can fill in each middle circle before running the sheet off for your class. The author prefers dictating each rule (circle) to the class and reviewing their answers with their classmates. This will allow students time to compare their answers and expand their knowledge in each category. Ten suggestions for use of "Circle World" are completed for you. Answers will, of course, vary no matter what rule you use.

Ask the pupils to place an H in circle 1. In the circles around the H, they are to place two letters that will go with the H to make a three-letter word. An example would be OT which would make HOT. Fill in the rest of the circles with endings. Circle 2 has a T in it. Find three-letter words that start with T. Older classes can place TH in the middle and find words of varying lengths that start with TH but also have the short i sound as in **think, thin** etc.

Here are some of the many ideas you might wish to use "Circle World" to develop.

Each idea would be a full page. An example would be all the plural rules.

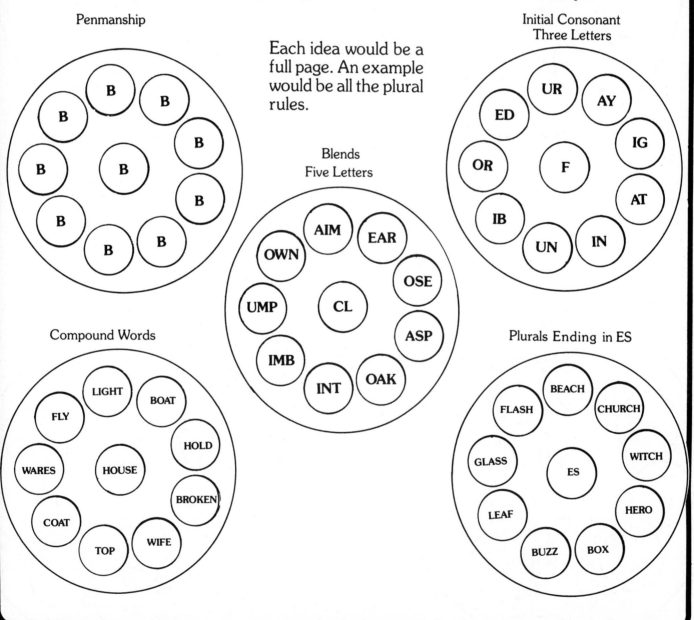

Penmanship

Initial Consonant
Three Letters

Blends
Five Letters

Compound Words

Plurals Ending in ES

Circle World
(cont'd.)

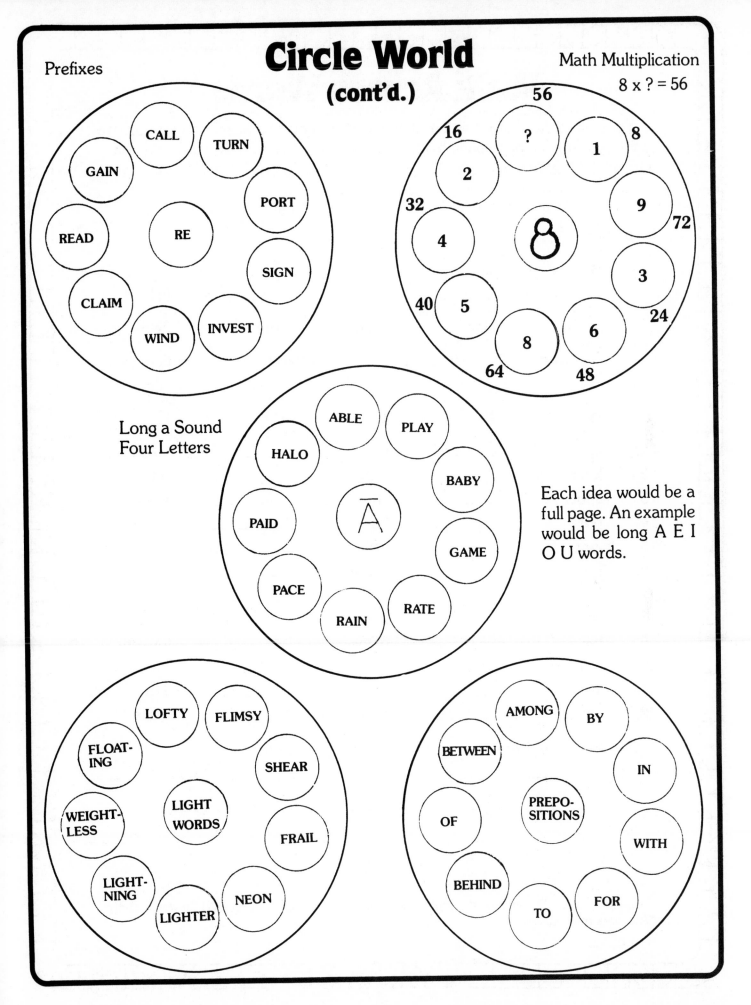

Prefixes circle: CALL, TURN, GAIN, PORT, READ, RE, SIGN, CLAIM, WIND, INVEST

Math circle: 56, 16, ?, 8, 2, 1, 32, 9, 72, 4, 8, 3, 40, 5, 24, 8, 6, 64, 48

Long a Sound
Four Letters

Long a circle: ABLE, PLAY, HALO, BABY, PAID, Ā, GAME, PACE, RATE, RAIN

Each idea would be a full page. An example would be long A E I O U words.

Light words circle: LOFTY, FLIMSY, FLOATING, SHEAR, WEIGHTLESS, LIGHT WORDS, FRAIL, LIGHTNING, NEON, LIGHTER

Prepositions circle: AMONG, BY, BETWEEN, IN, OF, PREPOSITIONS, WITH, BEHIND, FOR, TO

Walk Across Words

Your word flexibility will be challenged as you try to move from left to right by filling in each space below. If done correctly AB, BC, CD and finally DE will go together.

Example:

A	B	C	D	E
in	_____	walk	_____	field
in	side	walk	out	field
inside	sidewalk		walkout	outfield

	A	B	C	D	E
1.	light	_____	fly	_____	maché
2.	look	_____	cast	_____	set
3.	shot	_____	shy	_____	smith
4.	out	_____	back	_____	saddle
5.	key	_____	walk	_____	ward
6.	fire	* _____	proof	_____	able
7.	birth	_____	time	_____	cloth
8.	lemon	_____	pack	_____	trap
9.	base	_____	game	_____	for rent
10.	morning	_____	paper	_____	friend
11.	ice	_____	pocket	_____	dog
12.	cover	_____	friend	_____	mate

Can you write three of your own in the spaces below?

1. _____

2. _____

3. _____

Teacher Note: The critical thinking skills of your class will be enhanced by this activity.
*Answers may vary.

52

Historical Connections

"Historical Connections" is very much like "Walk Across Words."

The first historical character's last name is the same as the second historical character's first name. This makes a Historical Connection. Clues for each character will help you find the connection.

Character 1 Clue	**Character 2 Clue**
Example: First President/	Author of *Legend of Sleepy Hollow*
1. Greatest home run hitter/	Killed Alexander Hamilton in duel
2. Third President/	South's President during Civil War
3. Said "Give me Liberty or . . ."/	Famous explorer (N.Y. Bay and River)
4. *Poor Richard's Almanac* writer/	Three-term President
5. Holocaust diary writer/	Architect of great buildings
6. Civil War general (South)/	Killed J.F. Kennedy
7. Famous boxer "Brown Bomber"/	Discovered penicillin
8. World War I President/	Philadelphia's mayor 1980's
9. Wrote *Paradise Lost*/	Pennsylvania governor 1970's
10. Wrote *Ulysses*/	Wrote the poem "Trees"

Example:

<u>George</u>	<u>Washington</u>	<u>Irving</u>
First	**Last/First**	**Last**
1. _____	_____	_____
2. _____	_____	_____
3. _____	_____	_____
4. _____	_____	_____
5. _____	_____	_____
6. _____	_____	_____
7. _____	_____	_____
8. _____	_____	_____
9. _____	_____	_____
10. _____	_____	_____

Can you write the clues for these connections?
1. John Calvin   Calvin Coolidge
2. Upton Sinclair   Sinclair Lewis

Can you find two "Historical Connections" of your own?

_____   _____

Super Silo

Teacher Directions

Here are four teacher suggestions for using the Super Silo Blank Master.

1. Use the silos (A and B) to take your spelling test. Write the words you missed on the barn.
2. On silo A write the opposite of each word found on silo B.
3. Write the words for 1-20 on silos A and B.
4. Record some farm words on the silos that you'll use in a story on the other side of this paper.

*White out the above directions if you use this sheet as a work sheet.

A.

1.
2.
3.
4.
5.
6.
7.
8.
9.
10.

B.

11.
12.
13.
14.
15.
16.
17.
18.
19.
20.

Spell-Out Maze

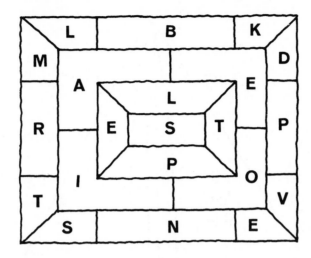

Can you start with the S in the middle and spell your way out of the maze, touching at least one letter on each connecting shape on your way out? Each letter must touch the next letter used. You may also touch a letter twice, such as in the word **sleep**. Another way to generate larger words is to spell your way out to the outside of the maze, then inside and out again. All these moves are legal if the letters in your word consecutively touch each other. Keep track of your words below and see if you can design a "Spell-Out Maze" of your own.

Four-Letter Words	Five	Six	Seven
stop	spine	spirit	stopped

Can you start on the outside and spell your way into the middle?

pots	deals	strips	kettles

55

Aye, Aye, (i i)

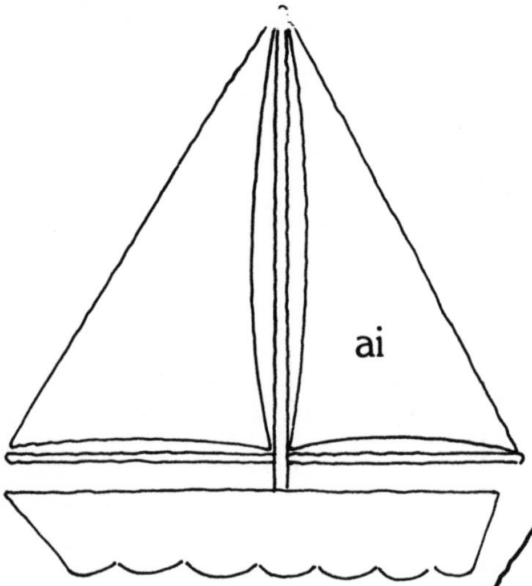

ai

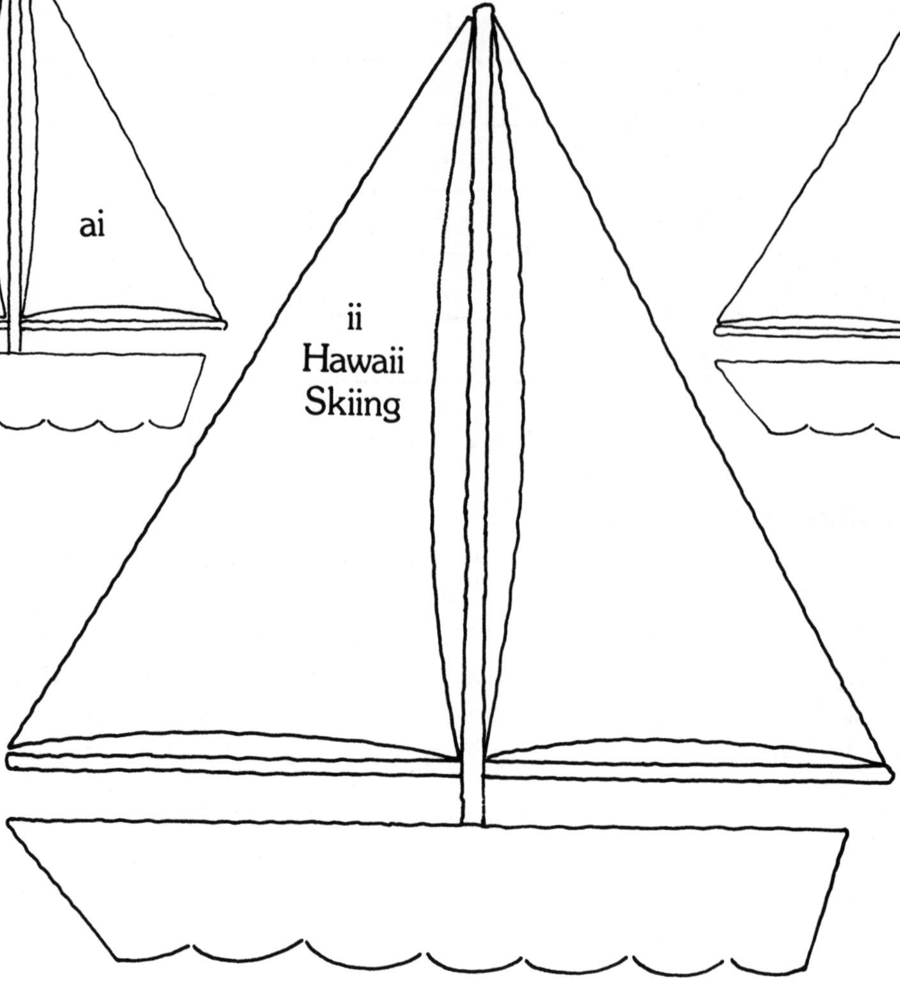

ii
Hawaii
Skiing

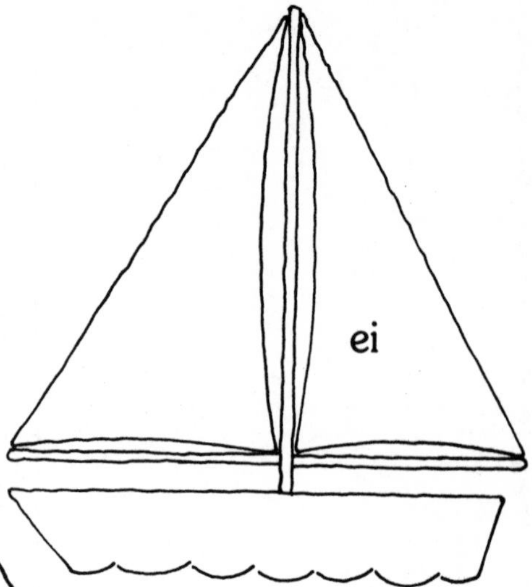

ei

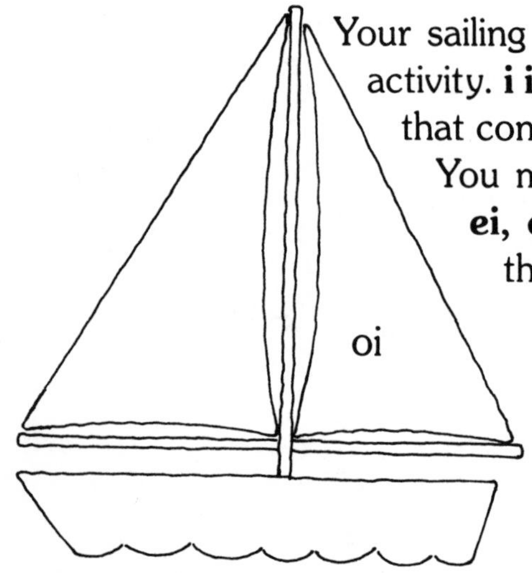

oi

Your sailing and word prowess will be tested with this activity. **i i** in the title refers to the scarcity of words that contain double i's, such as: sk**ii**ng, Hawa**ii**. You might have better success finding **ai, ei, oi** and **ui** words. Place the words that you have found by the appropriate sailboats and color in the sailboat when you find five words for each class. Answers will vary.

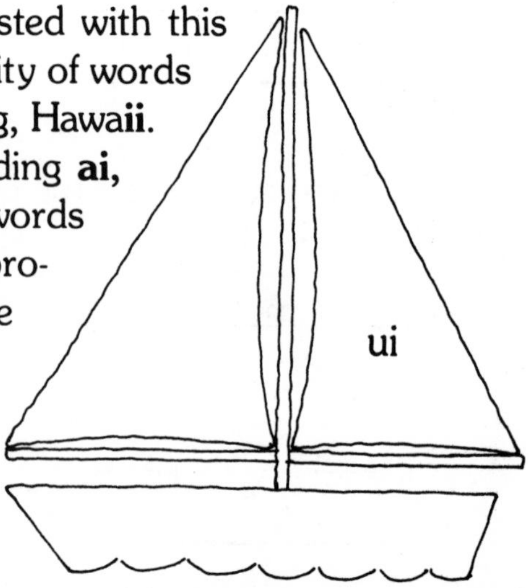

ui

 # The All-Purpose A B C Chart

Student Page

	1	2	3
A			
B			
C			
D			
E			
F			
G			
H			

This all-purpose chart can be used for penmanship practice, syllabification practice and initial and final word ending activities.

The All-Purpose A B C Chart
Teacher Directions

The ABC Chart can be used for the following skill development:

1. **Penmanship**
   Have your pupils point to the A on the left of their chart and the 1 at the top of the chart. In the box where they meet, one A should be made. Where the 2 and A meet, two A's should be made and so on. Pupils usually make a large A, then a smaller one. Encourage them to make letters the same size.

	1	2	3
A	A	AA	AAA
B	B	BB	BBB
C	C	CC	CCC

2. **Initial Letter/One, Two or Three Syllables**
   Where the A and 1 meet, a one-syllable word starting with A is placed; 2 and A is a two-syllable word, etc.

	1	2	3
A	ant	attic	animal
B	boy	baby	beautiful
C	car	caring	carpenter

3. **Final Letter/One, Two or Three Syllables**
   Where the A and 1 meet, a one-syllable word ending in A is placed; 2 and A is a two-syllable word ending in A, etc.

	1	2	3
A	tea	hula	formula
B	cab	Arab	catacomb
C	arc	topic	cardiac

4. **Initial and Final Letter the Same/One, Two and Three-Syllable Words**
   Top classes can be challenged with this modification. The first and last letters in each word are represented by the letter on the left. The numbers above still represent the number of syllables.

	1 syllable	2 syllables	3 syllables
A	a	aura	area
B	blab	bathtub	baobab
C	chic	comic	caloric
D	did	dated	detested
E	eve	encore	elevate
F	fluff	fireproof	failureproof
G	gag	going	galloping
H	high	hundredth	horseradish

Variations can be to find the smallest or largest word that would fit each category. Where the A and 2 meet, a two-syllable word beginning and ending in A is placed; where A and 3 meet, a three-syllable word beginning and ending in A is placed, etc.

I Get a Kick Out Of

Interest Survey

List ten things that you get a kick out of. Then design a logo for your pants and shoe before coloring it in.

1. _____
2. _____
3. _____
4. _____
5. _____
6. _____
7. _____
8. _____
9. _____
10. _____

Teacher Note: This activity will serve as an interest inventory. Future lessons can be based on each student's individual interests.

Which Floor, Please?

Please cut out the elevator and riders and move them to the floor your teacher calls out. The work sheet can be used to teach cardinal and ordinal numbers, initial and final consonants, and spelling if you put a new vowel on the elevator each time it moves between buildings.

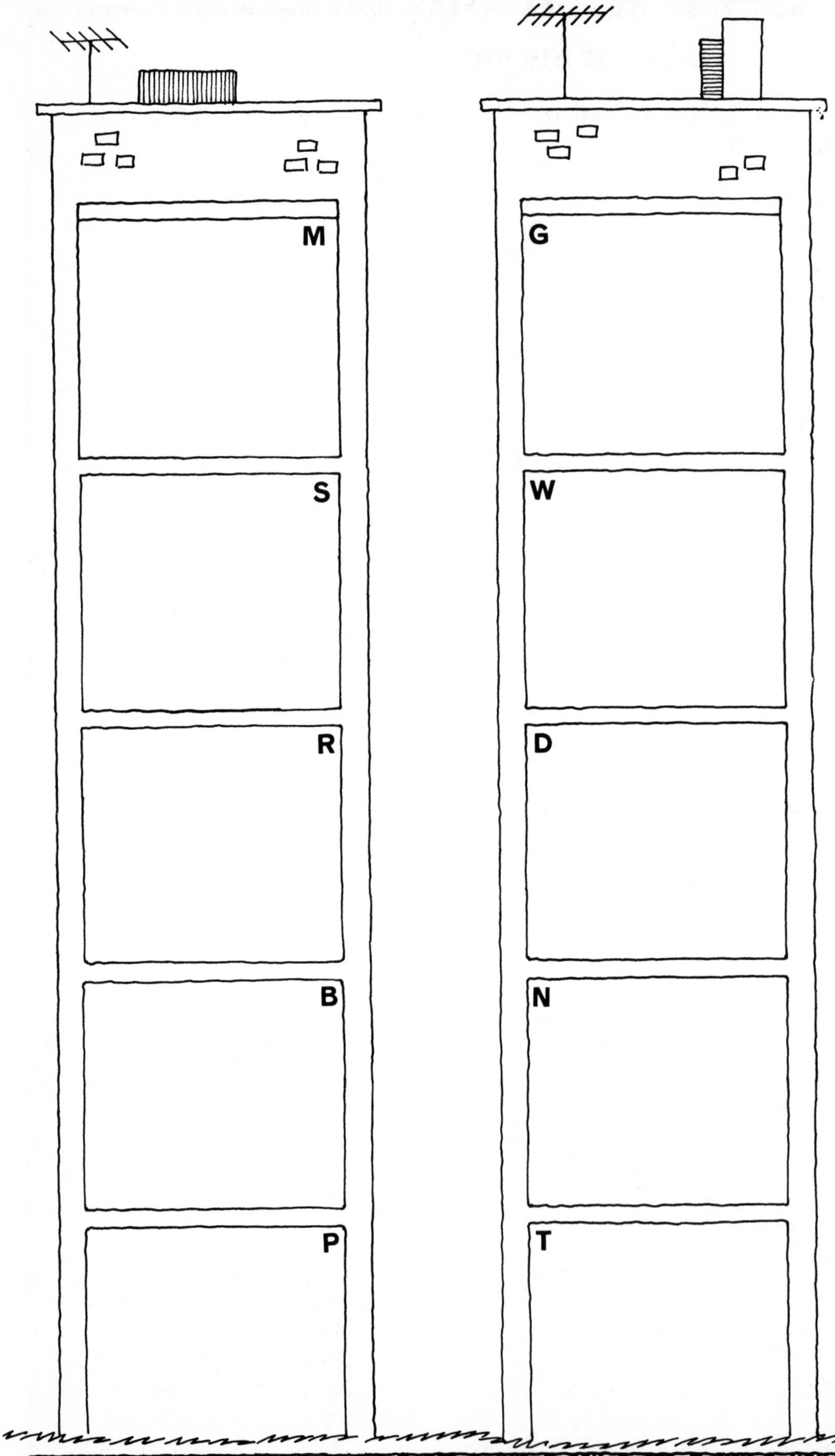

M

S

R

B

P

G

W

D

N

T

Build a Poem of Opposites

Help me, please, as I try to build a poem of opposites. Place a line of verse next to each letter as we complete this group poem. Answers will vary, so try to think of something that few fellow classmates will think of using.

Sweet and sour
I eat them by the hour
Big and small

A. _____

Fat and thin
A diet I can win

B. _____

Always on the go

C. _____

Not an expensive price
Bad and good

D. _____

E. _____

F. _____

Rigid and loose

G. _____

Borrow and own

H. _____

Beginning and end

I. _____

Try an opposites poem of your own. How about finishing or experimenting with a color poem?

I like blue . . .
A color that's true . . .
I think I said . . .
My bed is red.

You Are Too Young to Drive

You may be too young to drive, but you should know the words below. Cut out the car and drive it on the correct road. Your teacher will call out a word. Place your car on that word's road. Maybe your teacher will ask you what comes first in alphabetical order . . . last . . . after **go** . . . . Extra roads and words can be added to this driver's training work sheet.

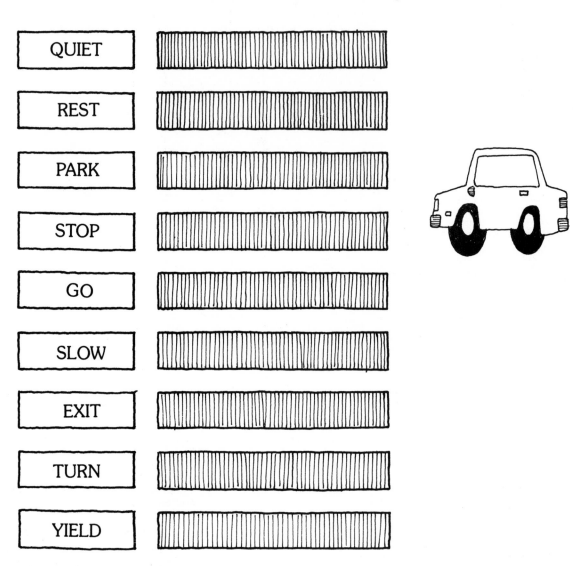

QUIET

REST

PARK

STOP

GO

SLOW

EXIT

TURN

YIELD

Teacher Note: Your spelling words can be placed on the left. You call out its definition. Student places car on that road. Younger children have used their own slot cars with this activity.

The Word Man
Student Page

"The Word Man" is a seek and find. The clues below will help you find words written vertically, horizontally, diagonally and around corners.

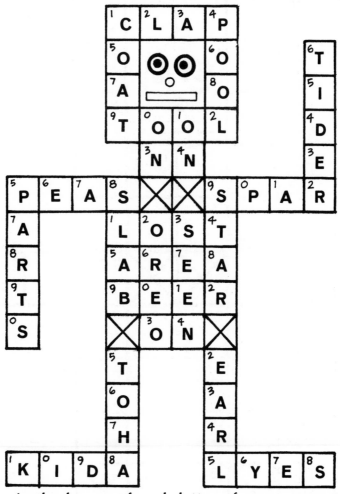

Add the numbers in the boxes of each letter of your answer and write the sum on the blank beside the word.

Example: A place to swim   <u>POOL</u>   <u>20</u>

1. A vegetable   _____ _____
2. A drink   _____ _____
3. A cookie   _____ _____
4. A state   _____ _____
5. A soap   _____ _____
6. Rug measure   _____ _____
7. A color   _____ _____
8. Pieces   _____ _____
9. Opposite of cold   _____ _____
10. An animal   _____ _____

Make up some hints for other words hidden on the Word man. Share them with a classmate.

1. _____
2. _____
3. _____
4. _____
5. _____

The Word Man

Blank Master

Hide your own words on this blank master.

Follow the X
Teacher Directions

Purpose: To teach how to follow directions.

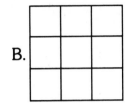

A.

3	1	7
8	6	5
4	9	2

B.

Place Chart A on the chalkboard.

Next to it put a similar but empty chart (Chart B). Inform the class you are going to name numbers with X's. Challenge them to find out your numbers and secret for naming them. Place an X in the bottom left-hand corner of Chart B. Call out **four** before anyone in the class answers. Tell the class the score is teacher one, class nothing. Erase the X and put it in a different location. If you know the answer, put it on your paper and circle it. The teacher then walks around the room surveying answers. Alternate between writing down and calling out the correct answer until the class seems to understand that the X corresponds to a number on Chart A.

Now put two X's on Chart B.

B.

x		
x		

You are now able to review and strengthen addition, multiplication, subtraction or division facts. If you wanted to review addition using this chart, the answer would be 12 (8 + 4) — subtraction 4 (8 – 4) — multiplication 32 (8 x 4) — division 2 (8 ÷ 4). HINT: You always divide the smaller into the larger. Later on this technique may even be used for fractions. HINT: The smaller is placed over the larger 4/8 = 1/2. Remember to keep your rules consistent each day, for example, only addition on Monday.

Work sheets using this technique can easily be made and given out.

		x
		x

= ?

		x
x		

= ?

	x	
	x	

= ?

How many different pictures and answers can you find using two X's? Challenge the class to some three in a rows.

65

First and Last Grids
Teacher Directions

The grids can be used to teach initial and final consonant sounds as well as eye coordination. Place the two grids on the chalkboard and distribute similar sheets to the class.

Chart 1

FIRST

LAST

Chart 2

S	G	H	M
R	A	E	F
N	I	O	W
B	D	C	T

Stage 1

Place an X in the top left corner of the first grid (Chart 1) on the chalkboard. Tell the class you have sent them a secret message. Can they tell you what letter you sent them? (The answer is S.) Erase the X and place it in a new location until the class realizes the relationship of the grid on the left to that on the right. Bring students to the board to locate letters.

Stage 2

Each student now makes and places his own X on the grid on the left as you call out letters from grid (Chart 2). Circulate around the room to see if pupils are completing each task correctly.

Stage 3

Using only Chart 2 and the first and last cover-up cards, repeat the same procedure, only this time pupils are to cover the first sound they hear in words you call out. Later this can be used for final sounds. The final stage helps students to cover up both the first and last sounds they hear.

Stage 4

Same Chart 1 and Chart 2 will be used. On Chart 1 label the locations shown below. Ask the class to identify the letters that the numbers 1, 2 and 3 represent. The answer is COW. Continue this with three and four-letter words. Ask pupils to come up to the board and number the blank Chart 1 with words they know. Have the class figure out pupil selections.

		2	3
		1	

It's Third
Teacher Directions

Purposes: To reinforce the identity.
           To review and strengthen vocabulary.

Explain to the class that each clue below will help them discover a word whose third letter is an A. (You may wish to substitute an easier task like words that begin with A or T.) After you arrive at the clue word, you can find your score for each word by multiplying the number of A's in the word times the total number of letters in it.

Clue	Answer	Score
Example: A color	orange	1 x 6 = 6
1. A state	Alaska	3 x 6 = 18
2. A cobra is one	snake	1 x 5 = 5
3. A boy's name	Stanley	1 x 7 = 7
4. A girl's name	Grace	1 x 5 = 5
5. A hockey player's shoes	skates	1 x 6 = 6
6. A reindeer of Santa's	Prancer	1 x 7 = 7
7. A shell carrier	snail	1 x 5 = 5
8. A fruit	grape	1 x 5 = 5
9. Horses are found here	stable	1 x 6 = 6
10. A drink	tea	1 x 3 = 3
11. Eve's partner	Adam	2 x 4 = 8
12. Happy	glad	1 x 4 = 4

(Answers may vary.)

You may want the class to write some clues of their own. Extend the activity as follows:

Find the value of
   your first name _____
   your last name _____
   your school _____
   Philadelphia _____

   Pennsylvania _____
   your favorite food _____
   your favorite TV show _____

Try to find the value of these math words. Your rule is number of E's times total letters in the word.

line 1 x 4 = 4
circle 1 x 6 = 6
geometry 2 x 7 = 14
mile 1 x 4 = 4
meter 2 x 5 = 10

gallon 0 x 6 = 0
quart 0 x 5 = 0
weight 1 x 6 = 6
even 2 x 4 = 8
prime 1 x 5 = 5

Pick a topic and make a list of your own.

Both Sides of a Name

A - 1   G - 6   M - 1   S - 6
B - 2   H - 5   N - 2   T - 5
C - 3   I - 4   O - 3   U - 4
D - 4   J - 3   P - 4   V - 3
E - 5   K - 2   QZ - 5   W - 2
F - 6   L - 1   R - 6   XY - 1

I. Each word below can be unscrambled into a boy's or girl's name. Use the chart above to find the values of the first and last letters in the name. Add these numbers for score.
   Example: YAM = **AMY** = 1 + 1 = 2

A. USE _____   _____ + _____ = ____

B. TAP _____   _____ + _____ = ____

C. ANTS _____   _____ + _____ = ____

D. END _____   _____ + _____ = ____

E. MOAN _____   _____ + _____ = ____

F. EVENTS _____   _____ + _____ = ____

G. GEM _____   _____ + _____ = ____

H. DRAB _____   _____ + _____ = ____

I. ROAD _____   _____ + _____ = ____

J. DRAW _____   _____ + _____ = ____

K. LIE _____   _____ + _____ = ____

L. GOAL _____   _____ + _____ = ____

M. CLAY _____   _____ + _____ = ____

N. RICE _____   _____ + _____ = ____

O. GRADE _____   _____ + _____ = ____

II. Try YONDER _____

    WANDER _____

III. Can you add three names to the list?

    1. _____

    2. _____

    3. _____

Famous Numbers
Teacher Directions

Explain to your class that numbers play a very important part in children's literature and *everyday* writing. Ask them to associate a number with each clue you will give them. Use the clues below and clues from your own reading program.

I. Explain to the class that there is a special number associated with each clue on the left. After finding the clue number, multiply it by the number on the right to find your score.

Clue	*Special Number	*Problem	*Score
Example: Snow White	7	7 x **13**	91
1. blind mice	3	3 x **167**	501
2. Ali Baba	40	40 x **50**	2000
3. Cinderella's hour	12	12 x **13**	156
4. *Hollywood Squares*	9	9 x **899**	8091
5. Two weeks' sunrises	14	14 x **14**	196
6. Hexagon	6	6 x **232**	1392
7. Square	4	4 x **212**	848
8. Pentagon	5	5 x **123**	615
9. baseball team	9	9 x **60**	540
10. *Charlie's Angels*	3	30 x **3**	90
11. Steve Austin	6	6 x **40**	240

II. Have the class design some clues and problems of their own.

III. Can you find five books, five TV programs and five movies that have numbers in the titles?

Books	TV	Movies
1. *A Tale of Two Cities*	1. *Eight Is Enough*	1. *Five Easy Pieces*
2. _____	2. _____	2. _____
3. _____	3. _____	3. _____
4. _____	4. _____	4. _____
5. _____	5. _____	5. _____

*White out these columns if you use this sheet as a work sheet.

G Is for Goat

Teacher Directions

Have your class cut out the G and listen to the words you call out. 1. If the word begins with G, place your G in front of the large goat. 2. If it ends with G, place the G at the end of the large goat. 3. Later place your G in front of the small goat that has the appropriate last sound in the G word spoken.

1. Initial Consonant Practice
2. Final Consonant Practice
3. Initial and Final Practice

Cut out.

G

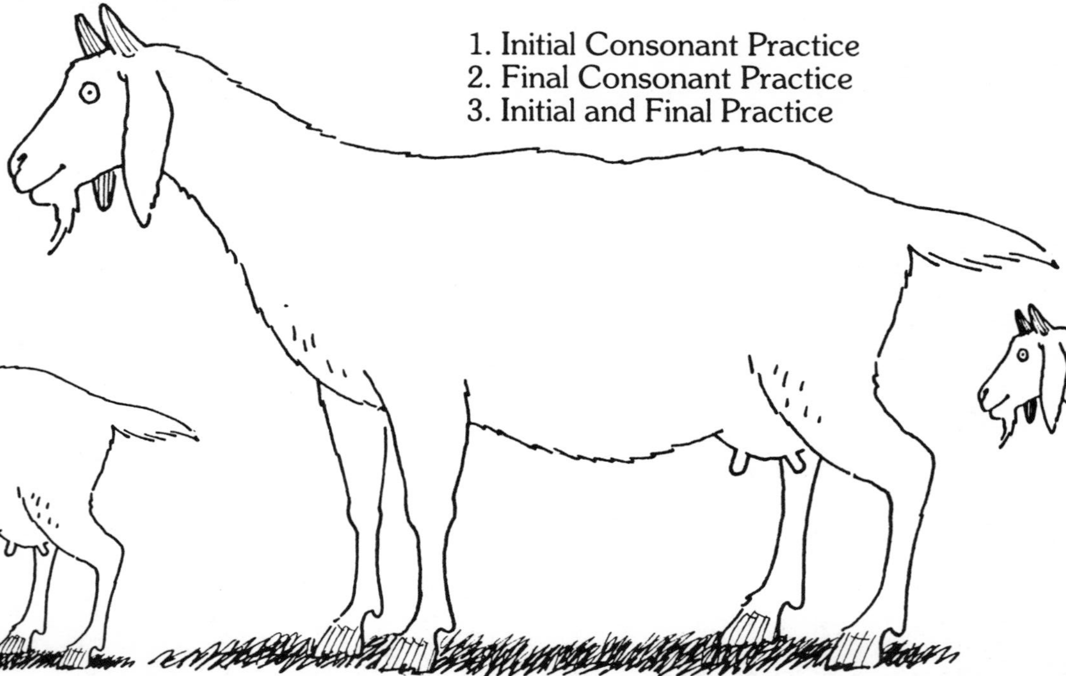

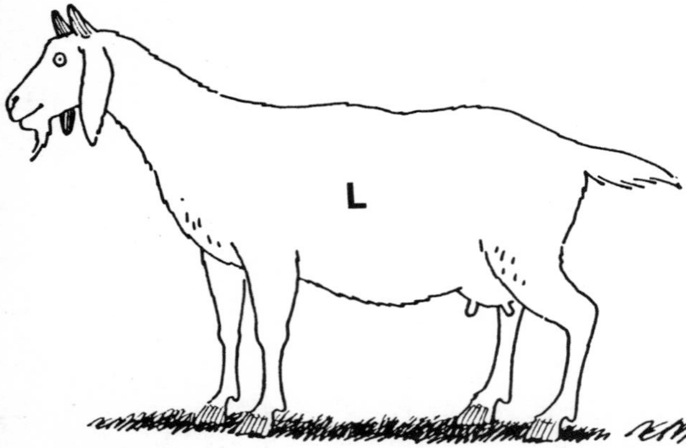

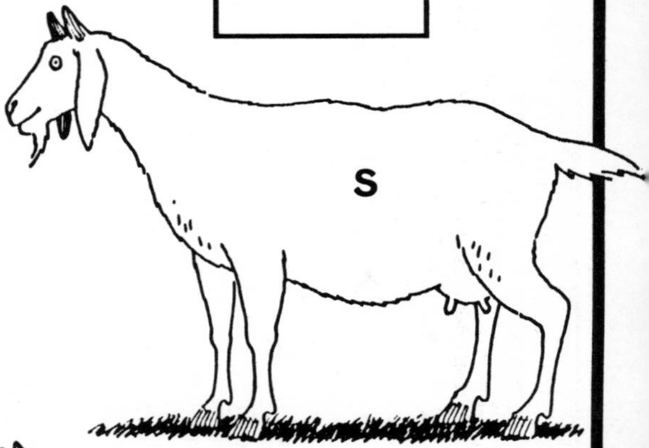

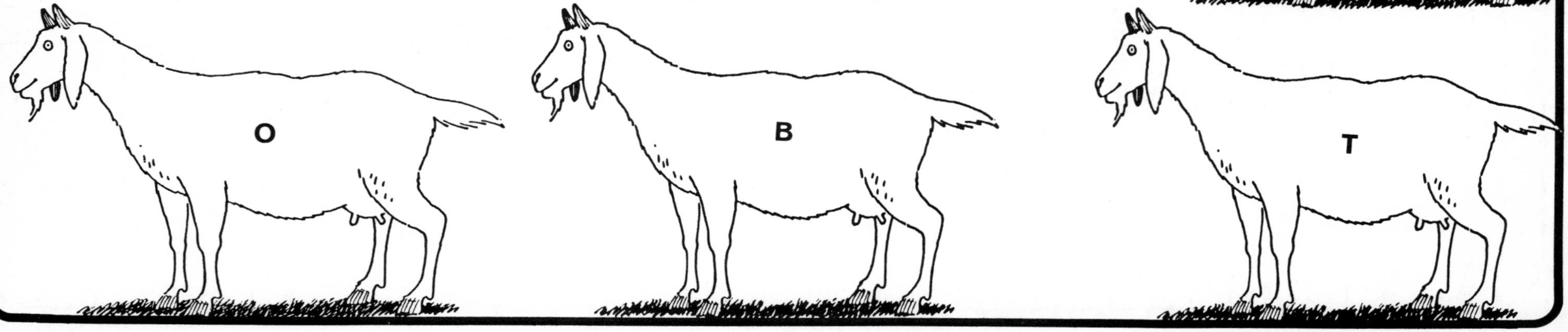

S

T

B

L

O

Word Mountain
Gameboard

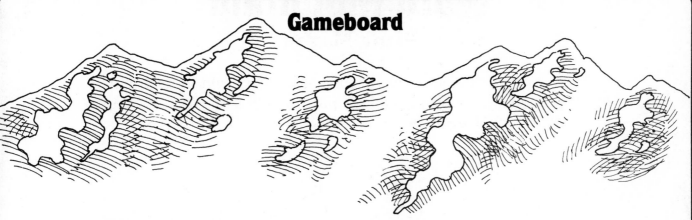

Place the following letters on a cube: B, R, S, T, C, D. Two teams start by placing their movers on the numbers 1, 2 below the mountain. In turn the cube is rolled, and if you can make a word with it, you may move to the lowest level of the mountain. In your next turn, you roll the cube and try for a match on the next level. First one to reach the top wins.

*You may also score points for every word you make on a line.

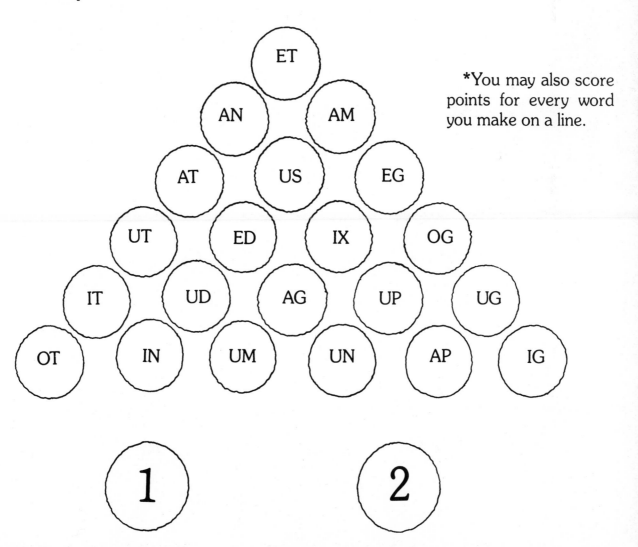

71

Word Mountain
Blank Master

Place three or four-letter word endings of your own in each circle.
Initial consonants or blends can be put on cubes or pieces of paper
in a pick-out box. Directions are the same as page 71.

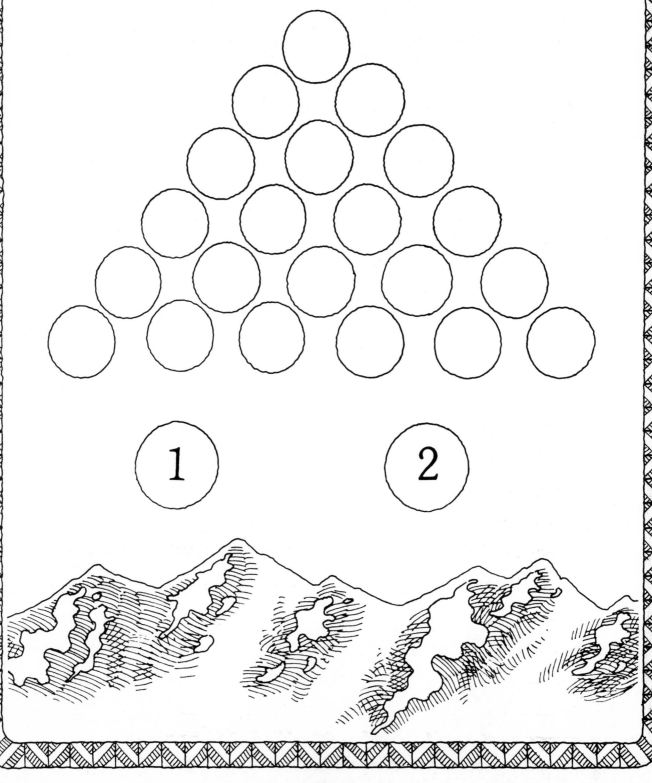

Colorful Language

Color is often used in creative writing to represent feeling or mood. These clues will make your writing more colorful.

I. What color is associated with these things?

1. Saint Patrick _____
2. Royalty _____
3. Old age _____
4. A baby girl _____
5. Halloween _____
6. A gardener's thumb _____

7. Planet Mars _____
8. Cowardice _____
9. Anger _____
10. Envy _____
11. Sadness _____
12. Robin Hood _____

II. Try getting these answers.

1. This is the color of the "flying angels." _____

2. This is the color of the hottest stars. _____

3. This car is in the most accidents. _____

III. Can you finish these song titles with a color?

1. " _____ Moon"
2. " _____ Velvet"
3. " _____ People Eater"
4. " _____ Submarine"

5. " _____ Christmas"
6. "Little _____ Apples"
7. "Nights in _____ Satin"
8. " _____ Brick Road"

IV. Can you write five color clues of your own?

_____

_____

V. Can you write five descriptive sentences showing the unique use of color words?

1. _____
2. _____
3. _____
4. _____
5. _____

Matchless Firecrackers

Teacher Directions

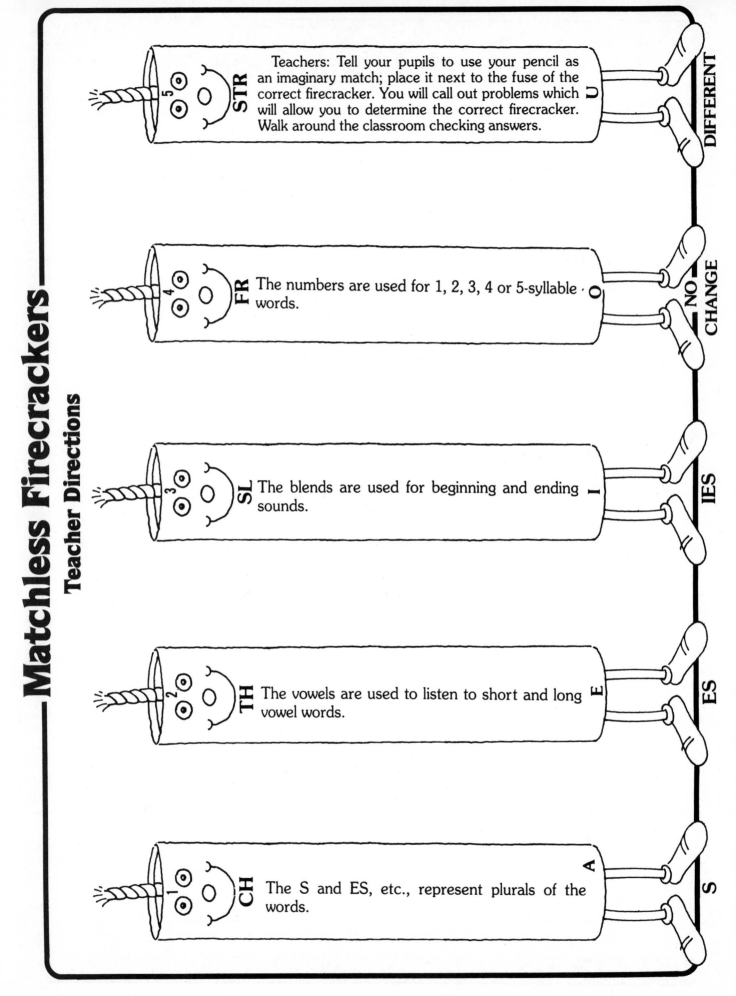

5³ STR U — Teachers: Tell your pupils to use your pencil as an imaginary match; place it next to the fuse of the correct firecracker. You will call out problems which will allow you to determine the correct firecracker. Walk around the classroom checking answers.

DIFFERENT

4 FR O — The numbers are used for 1, 2, 3, 4 or 5-syllable words.

NO CHANGE

3 SL I — The blends are used for beginning and ending sounds.

IES

2 TH E — The vowels are used to listen to short and long vowel words.

ES

1 CH A — The S and ES, etc., represent plurals of the words.

S

One, Two or Three Vowels
Student Page

Classification	One Vowel	Two Vowels	Three Vowels	*
Boy's Name	John	Lewis	Michael	
Girl's Name	Peggy	Sue	Elizabeth	
Color				
Body Part				
Clothing				
Meat				
Animal				
Game				
World City				
Automobile				
Planet				
Furniture				
School Subject				
Disease				
*				
*				
*				
*				
*				

I. Can you finish each category with a word that has only one vowel, then only two vowels and finally three and only three vowels?

II. Can you place your own classification next to the asterisks and complete each grid?

III. Can you write a sentence with a word which has one vowel? Two vowels? Three vowels?

1. _____

2. _____

3. _____

One, Two or Three Vowels
Teacher Directions

This chart will help your class develop a larger vocabulary and give them practice in vowel usage. Tell your class that the left side of the chart tells them the category. For each category they must find a word with only one vowel, then only two vowels and then only three vowels. This activity will not consider Y and W as vowels.

Classification	One-Vowel Words	Two-Vowel Words	Three-Vowel Words
Color	Red	Yellow	Orange
Body Part	Arm	Head	Appendix
Clothing	Scarf	Tie	Blouse
Meat	Ham	Steak	Salami
Animal	Cat	Otter	Beaver
Game	Tag	Bingo	Jump Rope
World City	Perth	Moscow	Chicago
Automobile	Ford	Porsche	Pontiac
Planet	Mars	Mercury	Uranus
Furniture	Bed	Couch	Armchair
School Subject	Art	English	Science
Disease	Mumps	Cancer	Measles

Answers will vary. The student chart has a fourth column and blanks for your own categories. Long vowel words can be encouraged for each category. This will make the chart more difficult.

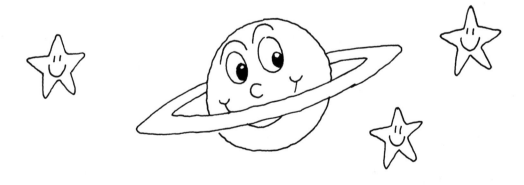

Three-Prop Poetry

Select a poem for recitation. Review the poem's significance, the author's thoughts about the poem and your feelings after reading your selection. Select three props that are significant to the poem, the author or to your feelings. Explain each prop's significance in the boxes below. Copy your poem on the back of this page.

Title of Poem _____ Author _____

Significance of Prop 1	Significance of Prop 2	Significance of Prop 3
My prop is _____ because . . .	My prop is _____ because . . .	My prop is _____ because . . .

Teacher Note: A list of poems can be given to the class, or students may pick poems of their own. The author suggests having students memorize their poems. You may want to just have them read. Cover a table with a tablecloth. Tell your class that at poetry readings three items are selected and placed on the table to convey the meaning of the poem.

After the student selects his poem, he should pick three items (made or found) that represent the poem, author or reciter and place them on the table for his recitation. After performing the poem, he explains to the class the significance of each item.

White out these teacher directions if you use this sheet as a work sheet.

Place Value and Spelling Abacus

Purposes: To reinforce charts and graphs.
To practice spelling.

Place the following abacus on the board.

	hundreds	tens	ones
9	A	S	B
8	S	U	N
7	T	I	E
6	C	A	T
5	O	L	S
4	L	E	M
3	E	T	D
2	B	O	G
1	R	R	A
		W	P

Place this problem on the chalkboard

$$14 \times 2$$

Ask for class assistance in solving it. After the answer is determined to be 28, ask the class to locate it on the abacus. The secret is ON. Have the class figure how this was determined.

Using an abacus, have the class try the following. Each answer should be stacked then added.

Clue	Word	Value
Example: A part of the body	arm	900
		10
		4
		914

1. A color (143)
2. A boy's name (724)
3. A girl's name (447)
4. A metal (778)
5. You take a bath in this (789)
6. Comes after nine (748)
7. You sleep in this (243)
8. Opposite of walk (188)

Have the class give clues for words they have found. The person who answers should give its place value.

Hungry for Language

Many words contain things we eat in them. Write the food answers in the blanks provided in the activity below.

I. What foods are hidden in the words below?

1. doughnut _____
2. corner_____
3. begging_____
4. appear_____
5. bundle_____

6. scrapple _____
7. startle _____
8. scrabble _____
9. copier _____
10. curdle _____

II. Can you think of words that contain these foods?

1. fig_____
2. meat _____
3. tea _____
4. ham _____

5. ice _____
6. sauce_____
7. pea_____
8. bean _____

III. Can you find six words that have foods hidden in them?

1._____
2._____
3._____

4._____
5._____
6._____

IV. Can you find six words that have names of people hidden in them (cotton-Otto, tomato-Tom, lever-Eve)?

1._____
2._____
3._____

4._____
5._____
6._____

You will need one die and one mover. Two players will alternate turns throwing the die and moving the marker. You may travel in any direction at any time. Land on a blend. Cross out a word part below that will combine with your blend to make a word. Play continues until a column is completed.

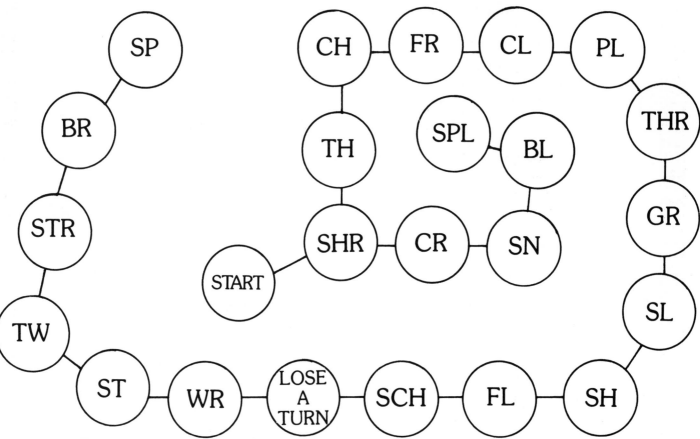

The last person to cross out a word piece in that column is the winner. You may cross out word pieces in any column.

EER	AME	OOD	OUR	IGHT	AN	UTE	ORM
AIL	ANET	ELF	AKE	ED	AIN	IM	EED
ING	OKE	AT	OWN	AIN	OAD	AG	AKE
OOL	EASE	OWER	IP	EAST	IME	UB	ET
URN	IST	IB	AME	AB	UD	OUD	URT
OT	IN	UP	EET	EAM	ILE	UG	ALP
1	2	3	4	5	6	7	8

Teachers should have the players keep track of the words they have crossed out on a 3" x 5" card.

Top Off Blends

You can "top off" each group of word fragments by placing two letters above the line that will form a word with each fragment below it.

Examples: _____   Answer: ___Sp_____   Words: Spice, Space,
          ice   ace   are   ice   ace   are   Spare

1. _____
   ore   are   air

2. _____
   ip   at   en

3. _____
   eam   ive   ess

4. _____
   eap   eer   ain

5. _____
   ag   ip   at

6. _____
   at   in   en

7. _____
   ot   ow   ue

8. _____
   an   ow   ay

9. _____
   own   ear   ean

10. _____
   out   ine   ore

Can you write five of your own to share with a classmate? Place your choices below.

1. _____

2. _____

3. _____

4. _____

5. _____

Give These Words a Tumble

Please cut out the gymnastic team members on this page. Listen to the word your teacher will emphasize in each sentence and place the correct tumbler on the mat. The sheet is set up for parts of speech, but any idea that children have to recognize can be put on the gymnasts' outfits.

CAT
VERY
MAN
REALLY
WITH
SICK
ON
BIG
HOUSE
PRETTY
FOOD
INTO
OFTEN

What Is Dialogue?

Start this activity with a discussion of dialogue. Good dialogue is important to creative writing. One thing that these two toucans can do is talk. Sometimes they run out of things to say. Can you help them talk to teach other using the spaces provided below? Remember that you are trying to make a conversation that goes back and forth between the two birds.

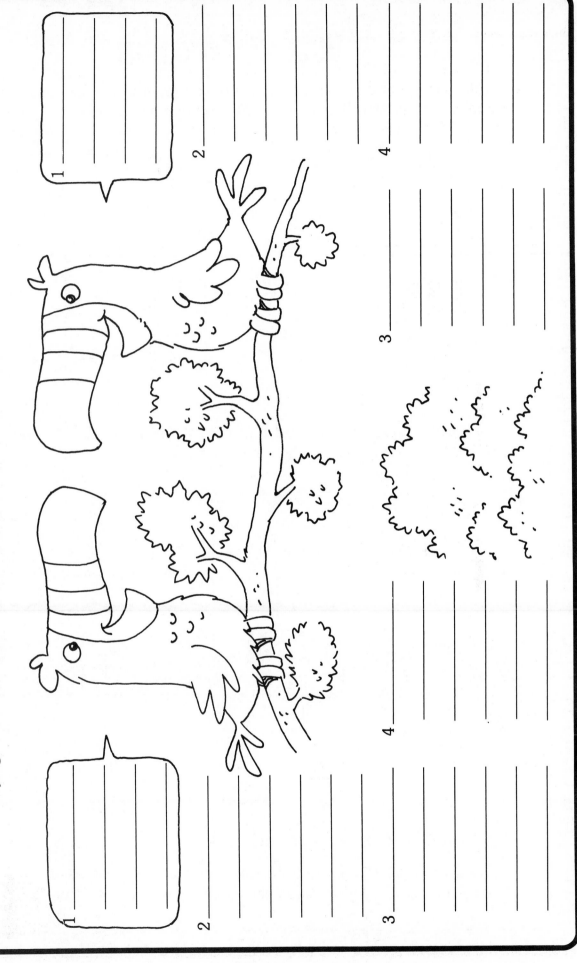

Word Drums

Use your pencil as a drumstick. Quietly tap the correct drum as your teacher calls out words whose initial letters are on each drum.

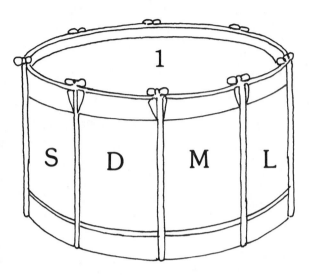

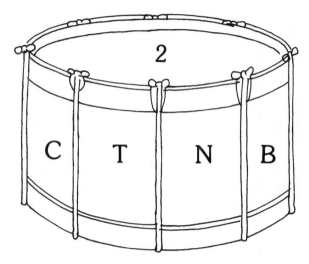

Cut out **Florence** and **Fred** and hold them up to go with the FL and FR words you hear your teacher pronounce.

Collect FL and FR words on the blanks.

Teacher Note: The 1 and 2 on the drums can also be used for one and two-syllable words. The children can again tap the correct drum.

Vowel Van

The Vowel Van Company is a special type of delivery service. It delivers vowels to the middle and ends words that need them. As your teacher calls out words, select the correct vowels to put in your van. Color and design your van after your vowel work is completed.

Teacher Note: Anything in language arts can be placed on the cutout boxes.

85

People, Paddles and Canoes

Your teacher will call out a person's name. Use the cutout paddle below to locate the canoe that the called-out person will use. After the activity is over, write five people's names in or around each canoe. The names should begin with the indicated letters.

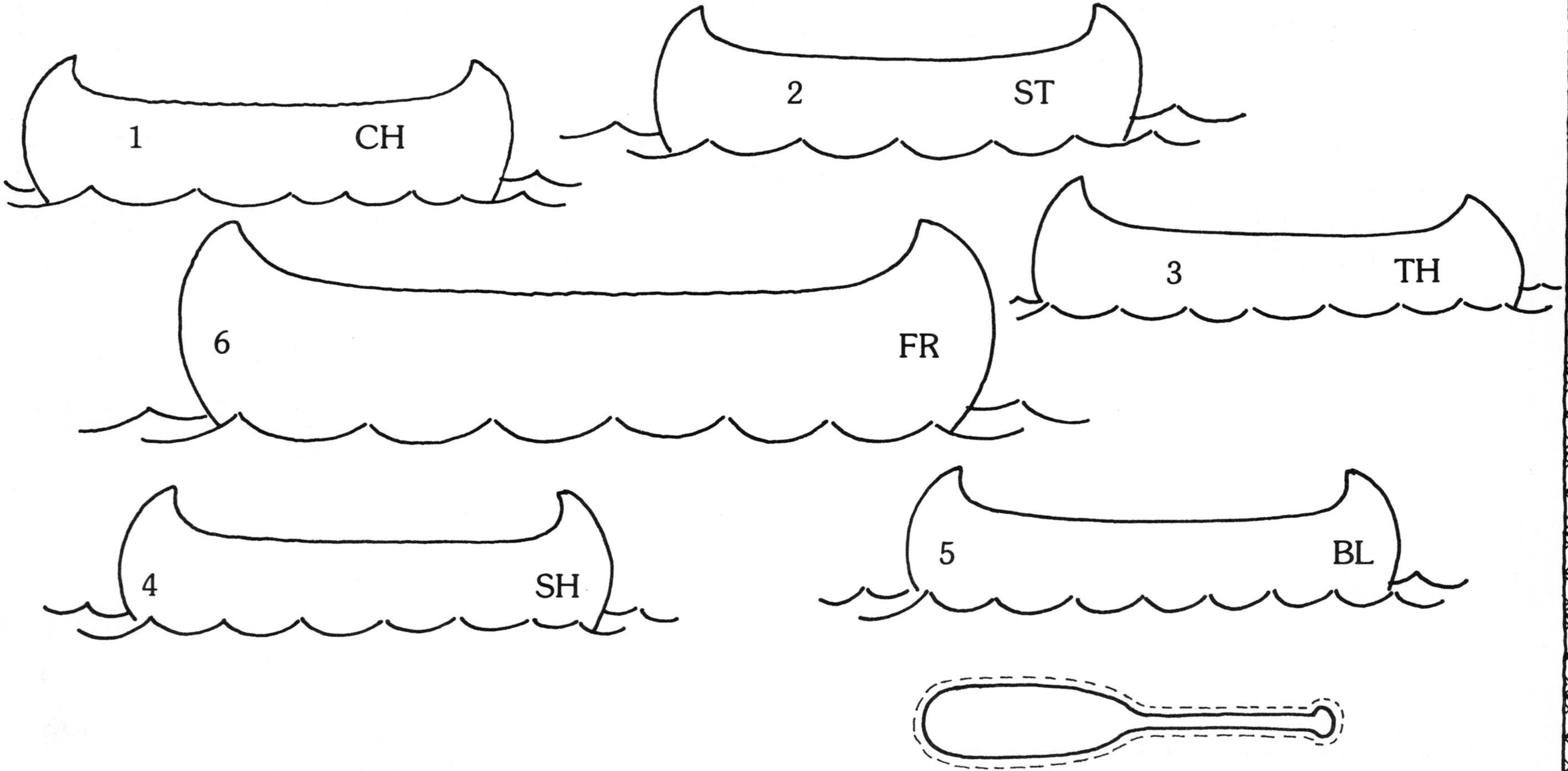

ST

2

CH

1

TH

3

FR

6

BL

5

SH

4

Teacher Note: The activity could be called "Punctuation Paddles." If you placed a punctuation mark in the middle of each boat, children would listen to sentences and then place the paddle with the correct canoe.

86

Dictation Board

Spelling Words

Short Story

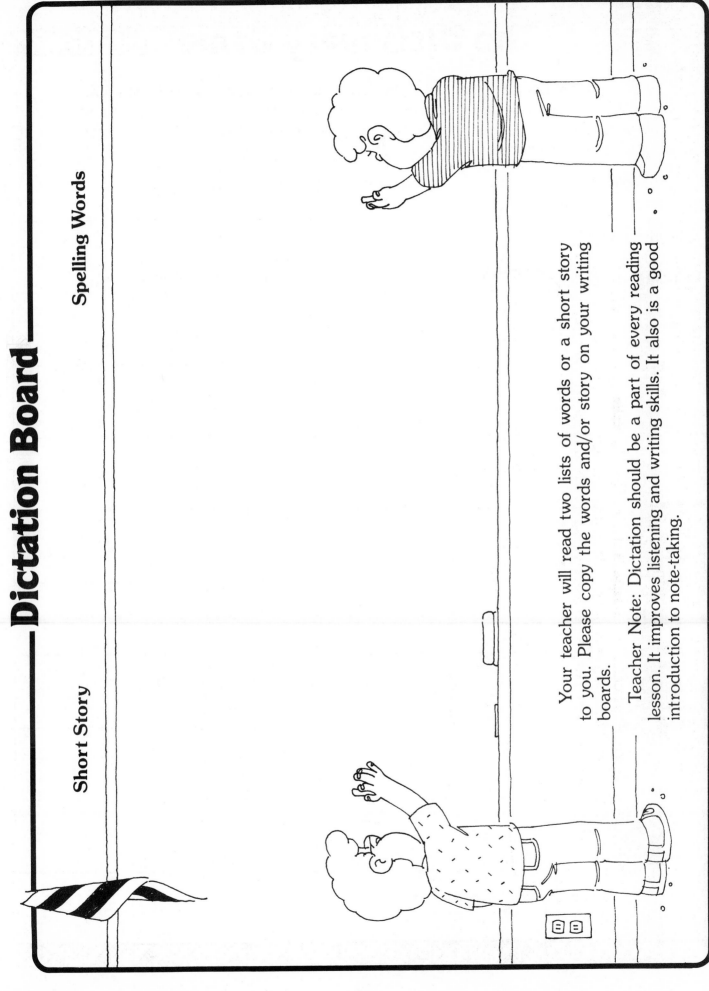

Your teacher will read two lists of words or a short story to you. Please copy the words and/or story on your writing boards.

Teacher Note: Dictation should be a part of every reading lesson. It improves listening and writing skills. It also is a good introduction to note-taking.

 # The Dictionary Game

Pick eight words from the dictionary that you feel no one else will know. Write the real definition and a fake one. Give this sheet to a friend and score ten points for each one you fool him/her on. This sheet can be exchanged with other classmates.

Writer _____   Challenger _____

Word	Example:	
*Maillot	an African bird	a swimming suit
_____	1.	
_____	2.	
_____	3.	
_____	4.	
_____	5.	
_____	6.	
_____	7.	
_____	8.	

*If you checked "an African bird," you are incorrect.

A Look at My Favorite Book

Many schools and classrooms have Favorite Book Days to introduce and display unique old and new books. Use this work sheet to attract someone to your favorite book. Use colored pencils, crayons or pictures to brighten this page. Set up a table of favorite books with this sheet next to each book selected by people in your class.

Title and Author

Setting

Favorite Character

Best Scene

Design for Book

Good Follow-Up Book

Book Would Appeal to

Tom Palumbo's Bookcase
Broadeners

Title	Author
1. *East of the Sun—West of the Moon*	Mercer Mayer
2. *Where the Wild Things Are*	Maurice Sendak
3. *Outside over There*	Maurice Sendak
4. *I Wish I Had a Computer That Makes Waffles*	Fitzhugh Dodson
5. *On Beyond Zebra*	Dr. Seuss
6. *The Lorax*	Dr. Seuss
7. *Tiger Eyes*	Judy Blume
8. *If I Were in Charge of the World*	Judith Viorst
9. *Where the Sidewalk Ends*	Shel Silverstein
10. *A Light in the Attic*	Shel Silverstein
11. *Leo the Late Bloomer*	Robert Kraus
12. *The Children's Story*	James Clavell
13. *Ramona Quimby—Age 8*	Beverly Cleary
14. *Count Worm*	Roger Hargreaves
15. *Albert the Alphabetical Elephant*	Roger Hargreaves
16. *Ira Sleeps Over*	Bernard Waber
17. *Jacob Have I Loved*	Katherine Paterson
18. *Bridge to Terabithia*	Katherine Paterson
19. *Encyclopedia Brown*	Donald Sobol
20. *The Trumpet of the Swan*	E. B. White
21. *Professor Diggins Dragons*	Felice Holman
22. *A Fly Went By*	Mike McClintock
23. *Just for You*	Mercer Mayer
24. *Just Me and My Dad*	Mercer Mayer
25. *Little Monster's Alphabet Book*	Mercer Mayer
26. *From the Mixed Up Files of Basil E. Frankweiler*	E. L. Konigsburg
27. *The Phantom Tollbooth*	Norton Juster
28. *The Chocolate Touch*	Patrick Catling
29. *Keep Your Mouth Closed Dear*	Aliki
30. *The King Who Rained*	Fred Gwynne
31. *The Cat Ate My Gymsuit*	Paula Danzinger
32. *Choose Your Own Adventure (Sahara)*	D. Terman
33. *Gates to Excellence*	Katherine Paterson
34. *A Wrinkle in Time*	Madelaine L'Engle
35. *Sadako and the Thousand Paper Cranes*	Eleanor Coerr
36. *Friends of the Loony Lake Monster*	Frank Bonham

These books are ideal additions to discussions of What Makes a Good Book. Each has a unique approach to children and literature.

Answer Key

Page 10

A. 1. fare
2. hire
3. hate
4. harp
Total: 10

B. 1. atop
2. shop
3. step
4. stow
Total: 10

C. 1. push
2. mash
3. much
4. must
Total: 10

D. 1. polo
2. silo
3. so-so
4. sold
Total: 10

E. 1.
2. shore
3. stare
4. stole
5. stork
Total: 14

F. 1. brain
2. t'wain
3. tryin'
4.
5. trait
Total: 11

G. 1.
2. share
3. spore
4. space
5. spark
Total: 14

H. 1.
2. spill
3. stall
4.
5. stilt
Total: 10

Page 19

1. California
2. Yugoslavia
3. Christopher
4. Bernadette
5. Los Angeles
6. automobile
7. Washington
8. Presidents
9. newspapers
10. revolution
11. basketball
12. thermostat

Page 24

1. seesaw — 3 x 3 = 9
2. housecoat — 5 x 4 = 20
3. tree house — 4 x 5 = 20
4. everyone — 5 x 3 = 15
5. headlight — 4 x 5 = 20
6. holdup — 4 x 2 = 8
7. turnover — 4 x 4 = 16
8. handsome — 4 x 4 = 16
9. nighttime — 5 x 4 = 20
10. bookcase — 4 x 4 = 16
11. onset — 2 x 3 = 6
12. someday — 4 x 3 = 12
13. master-at-arms — 6 x 2 x 4 = 48
14. seaport — 3 x 4 = 12
15. walkway — 4 x 3 = 12

Page 25

1. eb — baseball
2. ec — scarecrow
3. dr — bedroom
4. yb — everybody
5. ns — inside
6. ls — all-star
7. na — teenager
8. du — holdup
9. as — seashore
10. ew — sidewalk
11. yo — tryout
12. ps — upset
13. ec — tablecloth
14. no — turnover
15. em — fireman

Page 27

1. on — off — 2 + 7 = 9
2. head — foot — 3 + 9 = 12
3. win — lose — 4 + 8 = 12
4. fat — lean — 5 + 10 = 15
5. sip — gulp — 3 + 7 = 10
6. up — down — 2 + 6 = 8
7. love — hate — 5 + 9 = 14
8. Adam — Eve — 4 + 11 = 15
9. aid — hurt — 2 + 7 = 9
10. end — begin — 2 + 8 = 10
11. in — out — 3 + 8 = 11
12. ride — walk — 4 + 8 = 12

Page 28

1. little (←) — small (←) — 8 x 12 = 96
2. present (→) — now (→) — 3 x 11 = 33
3. boast (←) — brag (→) — 6 x 6 = 36
4. belt (←) — strap (←) — 6 x 13 = 78
5. alone (→) — lone (→) — 6 x 7 = 42
6. lead (→) — direct (←) — 2 x 12 = 24
7. off (→) — on (←) — 1 x 13 = 13
8. seal (←) — shut (→) — 5 x 5 = 25
9. set (←) — ready (←) — 4 x 9 = 36
10. flip (→) — toss (←) — 5 x 13 = 65
11. slim (←) — thin (←) — 5 x 10 = 50
12. lease (←) — rent (→) — 6 x 8 = 48

Page 35

1. cherry pie
2. Devil's food cake
3. Oreos
4. Twinkies
5. rice pudding
6. vanilla ice cream
7. plum pudding
8. apples
9. tarts
10. Angel food cake
11. pound cake
12. cheese cake
13. carrot cake
14. lemon pie
15. peach cobbler

Page 36

1. close
2. wink
3. wine
4. twins
5. closet
6. wing
7. closed
8. close-up
9. swing
10. window
11. swindle
12. Wind
13. windmill
14. Windsor
15. Winnipeg

Page 39

1. secretary
2. escalator
3. irregular
4. purchased
5. operation
6. rainproof
7. eliminate
8. headdress
9. earthward
10. meteorite

Page 44
1. bullet
2. bullfighting
3. bullion
4. bullfinch
5. bullheaded
6. bullfrog
7. bulletproof
8. bulletin board
9. bulldozer
10. bull pen
11. bulldog
12. Bull Moose
13. bull's-eye
14. bullhead

Page 45
1. housefly 9
2. outhouse 9
3. housebroken 36
4. housecoat 16
5. boathouse 16
6. House of Representatives 225
7. housewares 25
8. warehouse 16
9. houseboat 16
10. bathhouse 16
11. tree house 16
12. household 16
13. housekeeper 36
14. enginehouse 36
15. on the house 25
16. lighthouse 25
17. House of Commons 49
18. houselight 25

Page 52
1. house paper
2. over out
3. gun lock
4. draw side
5. board way
6. bomb or escape read
7. day table
8. ice rat
9. ball room
10. news boy
11. pick watch
12. girl ship

Page 53
1. Hank Aaron Burr
2. Thomas Jefferson Davis
3. Patrick Henry Hudson
4. Benjamin Franklin Roosevelt
5. Anne Frank Wright
6. Robert E. Lee Harvey Oswald
7. Joe Louis Pasteur
8. Woodrow Wilson Goode
9. John Milton Shapp
10. James Joyce Kilmer

Page 63
1. peas
2. beer
3. Oreo
4. Idaho
5. Tide
6. area
7. red
8. parts
9. hot
10. bear

Page 68
A. Sue 6 + 5 = 11
B. Pat 4 + 5 = 9
C. Stan 6 + 2 = 8
D. Ned 2 + 4 = 6
E. Mona 1 + 1 = 2
F. Steven 6 + 2 = 8
G. Meg 1 + 6 = 7
H. Brad 2 + 4 = 6
I. Dora 4 + 1 = 5
J. Ward 2 + 4 = 6
K. Eli 5 + 4 = 9
L. Olga 3 + 1 = 4
M. Lacy 1 + 1 = 2
N. Eric 5 + 3 = 8
O. Edgar 5 + 6 = 11

Page 73
I. 1. green
2. purple/blue
3. gray/white
4. pink
5. orange
6. green
7. red
8. yellow
9. red
10. green
11. blue
12. green

II. 1. blue (Air Force Team)
2. blue white
3. red

III. 1. Blue
2. Blue
3. Purple
4. Yellow
5. White
6. Green
7. White
8. Yellow

Page 79
I. 1. nut
2. corn
3. egg
4. pear
5. bun
6. apple
7. tart
8. crab
9. pie
10. curd

II. 1. figure
2. permeate
3. steam
4. shame
5. slice
6. saucer
7. peasant
8. Caribbean

Page 81
1. st
2. wh
3. dr
4. ch
5. fl
6. th
7. tr
8. pl
9. cl
10. sh